CW00555595

STEPPING INTO MY SHOES

Dr. Catherine A Baudino

Copyright © 2022 Dr. Catherine A Baudino

Autobiography / Memoir

All Rights Reserved. No part of this book may be reproduced in any manner whatsoever, or stored in any information storage system, or transmitted in any form or by any means, electronic, mechanical, photocopying, recording, or otherwise, without the prior written consent of the publisher, except in the case of brief quotations with proper reference, embodied in articles and reviews.

Printed in the United Kingdom

ISBN: 978-1-3999-2761-1

Published by: Baudino & Co Ltd.

Cover design: Branding London

Editorial Production: The Editor's Chair

HEARTFELT THANK-YOUS

Practicing what I preach, I would like to thank all my friends who have put up with me during the creation of this 'opus maximus' and my numerous references to 'in the book...'

But a few stand out:

- ► Anna Basova, for her undying interest and positivity from Moscow.
- ► Anna Downey, Entrepreneuse and founder of Buzzbar, for pushing me out of my comfort zone.
- ► Alexandra Morgan-Thomas, for going through the initiations to Team Dr Catherine.
- ► Federico Meoni, for his youth, curiosity and enthusiasm.
- ► Georgia Varjas, for her on-going support during this journey.
- ► John Camacho, for being my longest standing (as opposed to my oldest!) friend.
- ► Laura Hurren, for our very special Scorpio friendship.
- ► Mary Murphy, for always being there.
- ► Melissa Lund, for being my partner in crime.
- ► Sara Neame, for her wealth of feedback.
- ► Sam Wood, for being my Palestinian brother.
- ► Sukhy Cheema, for being my alter ego.
- ► Susan Stewart, for her ability to listen and her unfailing support.
- ► Zena Everett, for her encouragement and input as a fellow author.

TABLE OF CONTENTS

FIRST THOUGHTS

Stepping Into My Shoes is a book that combines a fascinating life story, a broad range of thoughtful perspectives, and practical learnings for both life and work. Catherine Baudino writes with fluency and her story-telling is engaging and easy to read. Her fascinating and sometimes painful experiences are blended with deeper philosophical and psychological insights, which are delivered with humanity, humility and humour.

I hope that many other people will step into Dr Catherine's shoes!

Roger Steare, Corporate Philosopher and author of:

- ► *Ethicability: How to Decide What's Right and Find the Courage to Do It*

- ► *How to Do What's RIGHT*

- ► *Thinking Outside the Inbox*

- ► *How to be Good at Work*

INTRODUCTION

This book has come to be as a result of countless friends and colleagues telling me that I should publish my story. Not vain enough to believe that an autobiography would be of interest to anyone – let alone total strangers – I thought about their comments for a while and decided it would be best to combine my life experiences with some coaching reflections.

Throughout the book, you will recognise a few recurring themes:

- ► Imposter syndrome
- ► Resilience
- ► Beliefs
- ► Convertible Skills
- ► Control
- ► Perception of events
- ► Humour
- ► Communication

...all of which feature in both my journey and my 'life learnings'.

You will come to realise that I believe everything is inter-connected, even if they don't at first appear so. This book is aimed at challenging your perceptions and interpretations by inviting you to walk in my shoes for a while.

I was born in London to French parents, who did their utmost to control me and my life – even from beyond the grave. They were not cruel; only dysfunctional and should never have conceived, really (but then, I was an accident!). Like many things in life, my upbringing brought with it good and not-so-good consequences. My corporate success is, in great part, due to the resilience I developed because of their unreasonable demands.

My personal and professional lives are best represented by a triangle.

- ► In the case of my personal life, the triangle represents the Baudino family in exile (in Central London, SW1 – so hardly slumming it!). As an only child, my view of life and reality was certainly distorted because my perception was very much through their eyes until I was old enough to know better;

- ► Concerning my professional life, it goes like this. The triangle in my company's logo represents three significant stages in my life:

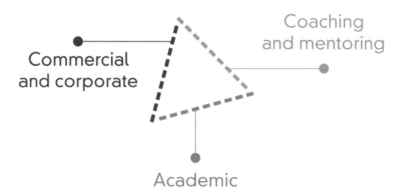

The base represents my academic aspirations. Once I realised that lecturing was not for me, I sped through my studies and obtained a PhD (in comparative literature) aged 23. It was 1976, and I was one of the youngest with this qualification in the UK at the time. From there (the left side of the triangle), I went on to the corporate and business world and, notwithstanding my literary background, managed to break the ceiling in 1987. I went onto the NASDAQ stock market and a venture of my own aimed at building solar parks in Italy.

At this stage (right-hand side of the triangle), I stopped all corporate and entrepreneurial activities and became a carer for my ageing parents. This lasted for a very painful nine years where, unable to take on any paid employment as a result of my caring duties, I took up mentoring and discovered I was quite good at this... I was eventually able to enrol on a coaching course and set up my business as a coach and mentor in 2010.

I am a keen reader of Marcel Proust, the author of *A La Recherche du Temps Perdu* (*Remembrance of Things Past*). For me, time is not lost; it is a source of reflexion (my deliberate mis-spelling).

The title of my book is a knowing wink to my shoe collection. My shoes are probably what people most remember about me! The title is also an invitation for you to look at the world (and my experiences) through a thoughtful eye. Have you ever walked behind a friend and tried to imitate their gait? If you have not, I invite you to do so. It is a fun exercise and one that will help you to see the world from their perspective. That is exactly what I would like you to do here and reflect on this new outlook on life, events and relationships.

Many of the reflections do indeed refer to women (I can hardly vouch for men!), but the subjects raised in this book are universal and I firmly believe that men will get as much out of this book as their female counterparts. For instance, I speak about:

► Elevator Pitch
► Imposter syndrome
► Networking
► Communication

In each chapter, you will find at least one invitation to ASK YOURSELF questions along the following lines:

ASK YOURSELF:

What would you do differently?

What have you learnt from this experience?

What advice would you give to someone in such a situation?

This reflects my coaching style as each of my coaching/ mentoring sessions ends with a Call to Action. It also encourages you, the reader, to reflect on the content and retain this book as your personal copy; a reference for your use and a source of 'reflexion'.

'The best effect of any book is that it excites the reader to self-activity.' – Thomas Carlyle

Join me on this journey of learning.

CHAPTER 1

HOW MY CHILDHOOD BROUGHT OUT THE REBEL IN ME YET TAUGHT ME TO CONFORM

What is your earliest memory?

Mine was not good, which is probably why I remember it!

I believe I was two years old, or so – but who counts at that age? I recall coming down with a mysterious illness that the doctors could not identify. I remember being very frightened, because I did not speak English and I was in a hospital for children in Vincent Square, Victoria, London. I lived with my French parents in Pimlico in a household where only French was spoken. My mother's mantra was, '*A la maison, on parle Français*' and, thus, it was.

In the bed next to me in the hospital was an overweight English boy who taunted me even though I could not understand what he was saying.

I recall my parents visiting me and asking me what I wanted as a 'get-well' gift. I asked for a handbag... I recall the bag so well. In fact, there were two bags: a large one that was white with red lining and a smaller, pocket-sized one also white with red lining. The large bag was larger than I was.

Thus my romance with handbags started at age two. This was later overtaken by matching shoes. My strange relationship with my parents also started at this time. It was a sort of trade-off: 'You do this (in this case, get better) and you will get that.' For instance, when, many years later, I was awarded a PhD at the tender age of twenty-three, my parents congratulated me with an expensive piece of jewellery.

As time went on (I obviously recovered from the mysterious illness), I went to the French Lycée in South Kensington, since renamed Lycée Charles de Gaulle. I now realise that this was the first time I went against the trend; whilst my contemporaries were British, Dutch or other nationalities, I was the only one in my class who spoke French. However, I did not speak English!

Whilst my schoolmates were learning French, I was becoming proficient in English thanks to our lovely teacher, Miss Thomas. This has resulted in my having, to my ear, a slightly plummy English accent; a combination of Queen Elizabeth and Mrs Thatcher. More recently, whilst speaking to a potential online date, I received the comment, 'You sound like Mrs Bouquet.' I had to explain that this was my genuine 'accent' and not a fake one. That was the end of that conversation.

When people would comment about my fluency in English, my father would (half) quip, 'It cost me enough money.'

So, you can also see that, even in these early days, my father (and equally my mother) put a £££ value on their contribution to my education, overlooking the fact that I won bursaries and scholarships for a major part of my school and university education.

I will later illustrate the pressure my parents put me under, not only to perform but also to excel. My mother could become quite angry and would frequently hit me. Such was the impact of her beatings that, whenever I saw someone raise a hand, I would flinch. That all stopped one day when I was about fifteen or so. The scene is so vivid to this day: we are standing in the kitchen; she slaps me on the cheek and I slap her back. Her stunned expression is embedded in my memory. And guess what? She never hit me after that! I discovered I could take control of a situation. By (literally) hitting back, I changed the dynamic between us from being a child to being an adult.

People often think that only-children like me are spoilt. Well, it certainly was not the case with me! My parents were certainly dysfunctional – they never should have conceived. I was informed at a very early age that I was an 'accident'. My mother had been pregnant once before and had undergone a very unpleasant back-street abortion. When she'd found out she was expecting again, she could not bear to go through the same ordeal. And so, I was born. I cannot remember how young I was when I was first told this story, but it was certainly before I could count or understand anything about the birds and the bees. Welcome to this world, Catherine!

The upside of being an only child is that you become an adult very quickly in life.

My parents had a property outside Menton and every year we would motor down through France, stopping off on our first night in the same hotel in Mâcon, Burgundy. Apparently, I would get out of the car carrying my little black toy cat and announce to the Concierge, *'La famille Baudino est arrivée'* (The Baudino family has arrived).

Arrogant, you might think. Or sweet, depending on your point of view. Your response will be coloured by what you think the behaviour of a female (or even a child) should be in any given circumstances.

One thing is for sure; later on in life, I was hired on at least two occasions for my 'gravitas'. I could talk to senior executives without fear or restraint. For instance, in my position as (the first) European Business Director for the NASDAQ market, I was able to

- approach leading business founders of companies like Olivetti, Benetton and Parmalat or political figures like Romano Prodi, Prime Minister of Italy, and British MPs such as Michael Heseltine and Cecil Parkinson, and
- secure face-to-face meetings with them.

This all came from my upbringing. The French have a wonderful word for it: 'formation'. For which I have never found an adequate translation. The dictionaries offer 'formation' or 'training' but I think it's a lot more along the lines of 'laying foundations' that will set you up for life just as a solid building is only solid if the foundations are secure.

In my case, because I was a swot at school (viz my ambitious mother), I was perceived as a 'safe pair of hands'. This meant that whenever a French prime minister visited our school, I was the one chosen to meet and greet. I think I was presented over a period of time to three or four French prime ministers, as a result.

Later in life, aged about thirty-six, I was invited to a dinner at Apsley House (also known as No. 1, London), hosted by Prince Charles.

Similarly, and early on in my life, when EMI approached the Lycée (my school) to select two fluent French-speaking boys and girls to produce eleven LPs (Long Playing records) over three months in their Abbey Road studios, I was one of the two girls chosen. Think Linguaphone in the old days or Babel today. The idea was to create everyday scenarios spoken in French and targeted at English schoolchildren studying the language. We would meet every Wednesday afternoon to record a programme about everyday life. My character, Cecile, would go to the market or prepare for her holiday.

These weekly visits to Abbey Road in the late '60s also coincided with the rise of The Beatles, Cilla Black and Sandy Shaw, whom I would meet in the cafeteria.

Even better than that, I got paid for my contribution and, being the swot that I was, I bought myself a desk with my 'salary'.

I hope these early recollections are not giving you the impression that I am bitter. My parents' behaviour has made me the person I am today and, if you forgive me for saying so, I (finally) quite like the person I am today – even if it has taken me years of therapy and self-analysis. Additionally, they were both bullies. Anne-Marie (my mother) would often refer to her husband as 'Hitler'. The upside of this is that I stand up to bullies – more on that later in the chapter entitled *Bullies and Boundaries*.

Because I do not want you to think I was this ultra-successful academic 'brat', I have to share with you the other side of these same EMI recordings. When we had finished the recordings, the Lycée's music teacher, *Monsieur Datas*, came to the studios to record typical French songs like '*Frère Jacques*'. With his back to the singers, playing the piano, he suddenly turned around and said (in French), 'There is someone here who is seriously off-key.' Well, of course, that person was me... So, I had succeeded with my speaking voice, but my singing let me down badly!

I went to a school where there were no uniforms – only dress codes.

I am aware of the pros and cons of uniforms. For me, not having a uniform meant that I gained an early awareness of dress and colour sense. It also had a side benefit. It taught me to be organised. Every night, I would lay out my clothes, books and accessories for the next day. This is a habit I have kept to this day! Not only selecting my clothes, but also preparing the papers I might need. It has served me well.

To go back to the subject of dealing with my parents; nearly everything with them was subject to negotiating with or outwitting them – no matter how trivial. For instance, I was not allowed into the kitchen, except to help with the washing up or to go to the fridge. Anne-Marie and René, who were both excellent cooks, thought of it as their domain and I was not allowed to attempt any form of cooking. So, I devised a scheme. Knowing that they both had a very sweet tooth, I proposed to make a dessert (which they rarely prepared and would buy in the form of a patisserie from *Bertaux*, an excellent pastry shop which still exists in Soho. My offer was accepted and I gained access to the sanctum of the Baudino kitchen. I proceeded to make my first-ever pudding: a soufflé Rothschild. It's a sweet soufflé with candied fruits marinated in alcohol. By following the recipe word for word, I was successful in my first cooking venture (phew!) and thus gained access to 'their' domain. I was eventually allowed to diversify into savoury dishes.

As with most negative experiences, the pressure to succeed also led me to believe that everything was possible. And so, at the tender age of seventeen, I embarked solely on a mission to confront the British academic system. I 'invited' university lecturers to re-evaluate A-Levels as the sole benchmark for acceptance to a British university and to accept a candidate with a French *Baccalauréat*.

To explain, in the early seventies, the *Baccalauréat* exam had not yet been recognised in the UK and so my application was not well looked upon. However, I fought and won a place at the top three universities in my application: UCL, King's and Bedford – all London-based (another story!).

I ultimately went for my first choice: UCL, where I obtained a BA and then a PhD in Comparative Literature in 1976.

As if that first battle was not enough, I embarked on a second although, as with the first, I had NO IDEA I was challenging the status quo. I truly, quite naïvely, believed that conversion from an academic environment into the corporate world would be seamless just as I had (again naïvely) thought there would be no obstacles between French and English school diplomas.

This time armed with this PhD awarded to me at a young age (twenty-three), I turned my sights toward the corporate world, unphased by my lack of commercial skills.

Oh, how I would have loved a coach or mentor in those days! Instead, I carried on blindly – only to receive recurring objections to my applications as being:

- ► over-qualified, or
- ► lacking in experience.

Somehow (and I know not why), I never lost confidence or hope. Is that courage? I do not believe so and, if it was courage, it was blind courage! Call it 'pig-headedness', 'resilience', 'arrogance', 'determination'. Aren't semantics a great thing?

I ultimately managed to enter the corporate world thanks to my languages. (I am trilingual in French, English and Italian, the latter of which I learned in my university years.)

I continuously rose to the challenge, but there was a backlash to my achievements. René and Anne-Marie were jealous of my successes. My mother would take great pleasure in belittling me and I believed her version of the facts. Unfortunately, though, there were other beliefs which were more grounded in my psyche. Anne-Marie told me from an early age that I was clumsy (*'tu es empotée'*) and I believed her; to this day, I have not completely overcome that perception.

She frequently compared herself to me in many other situations; at an early stage in my life, she declared I would never be as good a cyclist as herself, so it was pointless my going beyond stabilisers. So, now in my sixties, I have never learnt to ride a bike.

Anne-Marie also deprecated my dancing abilities, and thus I remain very shy on the dance floor (give me a boardroom meeting, rather than a dance floor, anytime). As Max Mason puts it, 'Beliefs create reality'[1]. However, they do not create the truth…

She would make out-of-the-blue statements to the effect, for instance, that her legs were better than mine. Whoever said there was a competition? And did it matter anyway?

It was a real Catch 22 for all of us because they wanted their dreams and unachieved ambitions realised by their only

---

1   Max Mason, *Stop Doubting Yourself* (Amazon, 2021) p. 21.

daughter and then me (not knowing any better), wanting to please them.

Their resentment and desire to control me, even after their ultimate deaths, is best illustrated in their Will. According to their testament, they left everything to me but my inheritance was to be left in the hands of three trustees – a man who sold kitchen and bathroom tiles and his two lawyers, for a further fifteen years. The reason for this was that, in their distorted view, I did not know how to manage money (even though at the time of writing their will I was European Business Development Director for the NASDAQ stock market!). I was not to inherit anything until fifteen years after their demise which, ultimately, would have meant that I would not touch anything before I was sixty-five years of age! Now, I have nothing against tiles salesmen, but I would have thought it obvious that I had at least as good a financial acumen as he did.

Mercifully, after much attrition, I managed – with considerable support from my husband, Alastair – to get them to change their Will, but it left a very bad taste in my mouth. Of course, their behaviour was not only an expression of their resentment of my success but also a statement of their desire to control me.

Fate and irony would intervene to reverse the cards, to some extent. Anne-Marie, who had been suffering from Parkinson's disease for a couple of decades, saw this sad, debilitating illness take a serious hold. René did his best to look after her, but he was physically weak, and she was a 'big lady'. It would take two grown men to lift her after a fall. Many a time, I would run out into the street to ask passers-by to assist me. I am amazed, to this day, how these total strangers would enter the house and come to our mutual assistance!

Ultimately, I had to drop a project I was working on (setting up solar parks in Italy) and take on the role of carer to her, and then, to him. This lasted for nine years – nine years of my life where I could no longer work, as I was on call 24/7. One minute, I would be making an attempt at normality, having lunch with a friend, and then I would receive a phone call telling me that one of them had fallen, or was in A&E.

I always marvel at the fact that the sick are referred to as 'patients' because they are anything but patient, particularly my already grumpy parents. The one who needs the patience is the carer! This was especially true of René, who would refuse to accept any suggestion of mine, on sheer principle.[2] A sort of cat and mouse game ensued, whereby I would find ways around the situation. One of my ploys was to get his visiting nurse to propose to him what I had in mind. For example, as a result of his incontinence, he really needed a plastic cushion to sit on, but he refused the suggestion when it came from me. I bade my time and waited for a home visit for the nurse to put the idea to him.

---

2   Similar to my recollection, earlier about being given access to the family kitchen [...].

Everything was a struggle. Any suggestion (made for their own welfare) was turned down, flat. Imagine nine relentless years of this. I, who had been this corporate executive, breaking down barriers and pioneering for herself and fellow female executives, ended up losing my identity. I ended up seeing a psychotherapist and remember crying in her practice, 'I no longer know who I am.'

My childhood has taught me that things may be tough, but they do not limit you; do not take 'no' as an answer. With the benefit of hindsight, I can now see that the constant, unrelenting need to negotiate, on even the smallest issues, with René and Anne-Marie has helped me in the workplace and has taught me to ASK – a predominantly male trait. Babcock and Laschever refer to a study conducted amongst postgraduate students of both sexes at a US university. It turned out that only seven per cent of the female students had negotiated their starting salary, whereas 57 per cent (eight times as many) of the men had asked for more money.[3]

Babcock and Laschever also study, at great length, the different behaviour of boys and girls. They point out the different signals sent by parents to their children. Boys will be rewarded for washing the car; girls will not be recompensed for washing the dishes.[4]

---

3   Babcok, Laschever, p. 1.
4   Babcok, Laschever, p. 47.

Our attitude to a negative response is equally often different, dependent on our sex and our upbringing. Men tend to shrug off defeat much more easily than women, who have a tendency to take rejection much more personally than them. Sue Unerman and Kathryn Jacob offer an interesting explanation for this. From a young age, boys play war games, in which they 'die', and then pick themselves up to live another battle.[5] Girls, on the other hand, play with dolls and learn to communicate and collaborate. This is a theme that is woven in and out of this book and we will explore it further later, particularly in the context of communication. I will speak further too on the subject of male versus female behaviour in the workplace.

I illustrated earlier how my childhood turned me into a fighter and, some might even say, a non-conformist, but I also need to share something very personal to me. My attitude towards motherhood. I have never had children, never been pregnant and never wanted children.

When Alastair and I were about to marry, he told me he had undergone a reversible vasectomy and would happily reverse the procedure if I wanted him to. I remember waving my arms in the air and saying, 'NO, NO, NO!'

This is often perceived as an anomaly for a woman, but I am quite confident about my decision and, if asked, attribute my choice to two factors:

---

5   Sue Unerman and Kathryn Jacob, *The Glass Wall* (Profile Books, 2016), p. 17.

1. Firstly, I was enjoying an international career, travelling abroad frequently and I felt that a child was a big responsibility and not one I could handle with my corporate lifestyle.

2. Secondly, my own experience as a child in a dysfunctional family had put me off the idea of having children. I did not want to repeat my parents' behaviour with a new person in this world.

These feelings have been so strong that I have also refused to be a godmother to any of my friends' offspring.

The irony is that children are often attracted to me and I am told I would have made a very good parent. I remain unsure of this and must declare here that, now, in my late sixties, I have no regrets at all, even if that makes me sound like a cold-hearted b****h! Before you view me, dear reader, as a selfish individual, I will also remind you that I gave up my career and my business to care for my two dysfunctional parents for nine very long years. That's longer than any maternity leave!

ASK YOURSELF:

In what way does your childhood experiences impact on your present behaviour?

CHAPTER 2

YOU ALWAYS HAVE A CHOICE AND THE CHANCE TO CHANGE

The best definition of *mindset* I have come across is, 'The manner in which you look at things; your perspective on the people and situation; the lens your eyes see the world through.'[6]

Before we enter into a discussion about mindset, I would like to invite you to look at this video, where three candidates are interviewed by the same two people for the same job: view on https://www.youtube.com/watch?v=f6k5i2AfPHA

ASK YOURSELF:

How, using adjectives such as positive, hesitant, winning, defensive, would you define the mindset (the perspective) of

- **Candidate 1**

---

6   Som Bathla, *Mindset Makeover* (Amazon, 2021), p. 9.

- **Candidate 2**

- **Candidate 3**

Few would disagree that the way to overcome obstacles is to gain a winning mindset, learn from each mistake, revisit your goals and abandon the setback mentality. Formula One racing car driver, Daniel Riccardo, wrote on LinkedIn following his comeback win at the Italian Formula One Grand Prix: 'Everyone faces speed bumps along their journey ... I try to acknowledge what brought me down and remember what my end goal is.'

His other tips include

- Ignore self-limiting beliefs to restore self-confidence.
- Remember why you love what you do and use it to fuel your actions.
- Try not to let other people's expectations or opinions drive you.
- Channel your negative energy into something positive.[7]

---

7   https://www.linkedin.com/news/story/how-to-cultivate-a-champion-mindset-5146204/

A soldier goes into battle not expecting to be defeated. In the words of Gene Kranz and the Apollo 13 Moon Team, 'Failure was not an option.' The impact of a positive mindset was highlighted by a US military official who commented that the Ukrainian soldiers' feisty attitude has been able to overcome the Russian military might.[8]

Have you noticed how many of our Olympic champions have overcome adversity in health to become who they are?

- ► Chris Mears, an Olympic diver, defied death with a burst spleen
- ► Becky James, a dual silver cyclist, had to stop training for eighteen months when she was diagnosed with early cervical cancer
- ► Siobhan-Marie O'Connor, a silver medallist in swimming, suffers from a bowel disease

And the list goes on.

It is a testament to how strong the brain is when faced with pain or possible loss of life.

When faced with things beyond their control (their health issues), these champions focused their minds not on the problem but on reaching their goals in their preferred sport. This, at least, was something they could manage.

---

8   11th March, 2022.

Furthermore, the thought of losing is not such a threat. Many of us lose in competitions because we have a fear of losing. The brilliant book by Susan Jeffers, *Feel the Fear and Do It Anyway*, comes to mind; fear of failure can literally paralyze. Thomas Edison is said to have commented, 'I have not failed. I've just found 10,000 ways that won't work.'

As a coach, I encourage my clients to see what they can learn from their 'failures'; as I encourage you, the reader, to step into my shoes and consider what you can learn from my experiences. In the words of my friend and business coach, Raimonda Jankunaite, 'Let your wounds be your inspiration, your story your motivation and your voice your secret weapon to inspire others.'

Once again, my childhood explains how I am not easily deterred. There was one time when, aged fourteen or so, I had a very high temperature (38°C) on the very day I was supposed to sit for a science exam. In Anne-Marie's mind, my health in no way prohibited my sitting the exam. Furthermore, I was expected to come out first in the class! So, Anne-Marie drove me to school to sit the exam and picked me up afterwards – and yes, I did get first place. I was not complimented on my success because, in my parents' minds, there was no other option.

The resilience that Anne-Marie expected of me has persisted to this day, but with a difference. Now it's MY choice. For instance, as I type this, I am presently recovering from a double fracture to my right hip (which has already been subjected to a replacement!). Realising that I still have other commitments, such as writing this book, participating today in a podcast, and seeing a couple of clients, I have recognised my limitations: I need to delegate some tasks that I am physically unable to complete. In other words, I have conceded to the support of a carer visiting me twice a day for a period of up to six weeks (the time it takes for bones to heal).

This may seem like nothing to you, my dear reader, but it is an ENORMOUS step for me... and another lesson learnt: delegate/accept support. In the words of Charryse Johnson, 'If I focus on being positive, everything else will take care of itself.'[9]

My best friend, John, who has known me since our uni days, says that I am the most organised person he knows. I am not sure that I agree, but it has certainly served me well to allow the brain to take over emotions. You could say it is what the former model, Gisele Bündchen, calls 'discipline'. She explains that, when dealing with her panic attacks, she concluded that when you are feeling sorry for yourself, 'you start seeing yourself as a victim and surrender your power'.[10] You have the choice to look at the situation differently.

Now, with the benefit of hindsight, I can see that I CHOSE to put that thinking into practice years before learning about 'choice/

---

9   Johnson, p. 159.
10   Gisele Bündchen, *Lessons* (Avery, 2018), p. 63.

reality theory'.[11] In this context, I will relate my behaviour to when, out of the blue, one day, Alastair, my husband, went out after breakfast and failed to return… After much pacing up and down, and rather than cry or wallow in my sorrow, I put myself into efficiency mode: I took out an old copybook, a pen and three phones which I placed on a tray. The three phones were two landlines, which I used for outgoing and incoming calls, and the mobile, just in case Alastair would phone me back.

The tray would follow me around the flat so that I made myself contactable twenty-four hours a day. In the notebook, I would jot down the times of my calls, the people to whom I spoke (particularly, the name of the police officer at the other end), the case number I was allocated, etc. This served me well, as I spent three agonising days waiting for my phone to ring with some news…

Don't get me wrong, I may have been 'operational', but I also had emotions; my voice messages on Alastair's phone went from pleading to anger and back to pleading again. Ultimately though, I was keeping myself together with my mobile tray; I was taking control in this nightmare of not knowing if my husband was still alive and, if so, in what condition. Mercifully, he was eventually found by a dog in a forest near Cambridge and ultimately survived.[12]

---

11   For those interested in this, I can do no better than point you towards Frankl and Reality Theory.

12   See reference 31.

No matter what the situation is, remember you have a choice. Elsewhere in this book, I talk about

- ► Setting boundaries (particularly in the case of bullies)
- ► The importance of saying 'No'
- ► The choice of HOW you are going to deliver that message
- ► The choice of WHEN you are going to deliver that message

Just the realisation that you can step back from a situation and choose your path is highly liberating.

Is a 'failure' a setback, or what? James Smith contends, 'A setback is only a setback if you see it that way.'[13]

I have explained earlier how I persisted as a young graduate to get my first corporate job and how I set up my own business as a coach, after nine years off as a carer. There is, however, one event in my life that I can neither forget nor see in any way other than failure. It is an event that caused me to lose over £100,000 and, more importantly, about £400,000 from family and friends, who wished to support me in a new venture.

The financial loss I suffered was nothing compared to the nightmares I had, trying to find a way around the problem. For legal reasons, I prefer not to say much more on this matter, other than that it came about by a third party who, yes, hoodwinked me. In so far as being hoodwinked goes, I

---

13   James Smith, p. 127.

am guilty and will always remain guilty in my view. I cannot do anything to change that; in the words of Shakespeare, 'What's done is done and cannot be undone.' I can, however, look back and learn my lesson: in this case, questioning a partner's declarations, even if they are from a close friend whom I had trusted in the past.

The link between mindset and perception is best illustrated in the Italian tragi-comic *La Vità E Bella* (Life Is Beautiful), in which a Jewish bookshop-owner-turned-waiter and his young son are sent to a Nazi concentration camp. Here, the hero uses his humour and imagination to protect his son from the realities of the environment by pretending it is a holiday camp.

Outward appearances also play a big part in developing a positive mindset. I, for example, will deliberately wear a bright colour if I am feeling low. A male friend of mine dons (some would say) garish coloured socks to lift his mood.

In his chapter on 'Mind and Medicine' in *Emotional Intelligence*, Daniel Goleman mentions that an emotion like depression '... has also been found to complicate recovery from hip fracture'.

Nothing could be truer than my own experience before my second hip replacement.

A lot of sufferers understandably feel anxiety over a total hip replacement. Additionally, many perceive their condition as a sign of old age showing its face. Whatever your age, there is no need for such trepidation. Nor do you need to be a fitness

Queen (or King) to overcome the operation. My story is proof of this because I have had TWO THPs (medical parlance for Total Hip Replacement).

The first was about fifteen years ago; I was run over by an errant bicyclist in Shaftesbury Avenue. When I came out of the theatre after having seen my favourite play in the world, *Kean*, with one of my favourite actors (Anthony Sher), the cyclist collided with my left hip. This collision ultimately forced me to undergo a full hip replacement.

Fast-forward eight years when the highly revered surgeon, Mr Warwick Radford, confirmed my worst suspicion; it was now the turn of my right hip. The reason for this is still unclear – perhaps arthritis, or, more likely, the result of a bladder infection.

Whatever the reason, the replacement was a given (my hip was two-thirds degenerated). Only the timing of it was up to me. At this stage, in January 2014, I was in considerable pain and discomfort. At the time, I had the privilege of having been chosen to mentor a veteran soldier suffering from PTSD (Post-Traumatic Stress Disorder), the most courageous Mark Taylor. I could hardly 'drop him' in mid-mentoring.

I decided to address the pain and get into an even more concerted exercise programme with my personal trainer, Michelle Cohen. Having discussed the matter with 'my' soldier, Michelle and Mr Radford, I decided the operation would take place sometime in September/October 2014.

The first obstacle was the pain. Practising what I preach, I sought to discover what I could do about it and whether the pain was purely physical or had another element to it – one which I could control.

After a lot of soul searching, I came to realise that a major component of my suffering came from my anxieties – not about the op, nor even the recovery but, in my case, the association with a very unpleasant incident that had occurred when I'd been recovering from Hip Op One.

To be explicit, my husband suddenly, once again, left one morning around week four of my recovery, without leaving a note or explanation. Three days later, the police discovered that he had driven himself off to Scotland to commit suicide.

The vulnerability I felt then was similar to the physical vulnerability and insecurity I faced before the operation. However, once I had determined the cause of my anxiety, the pain slowly declined as did my intake of paracetamol and ibuprofen. I skim over this part of my self-analysis as it is a story in itself to be told, perhaps, on another occasion.

As a result of this newfound awareness (i.e., the pain being emotional as well as physical), my entire mindset changed. I developed a CAN-DO mentality. I was going to fight this to the end and ensure that I would have a speedy recovery.

The pain and the fear abated and I set my mind to reducing the impact of the procedure on my lifestyle and recovery by strengthening my gluteal muscles (glutes), hip muscles, core (tummy), quads and upper body.

This time, the marvellous Michelle (or in her absence the equally Marvellous Mark Lucas at my Dolphin Square gym) established for me a pre-op preparation exercise schedule, which was suitable even for a woman more accustomed to boardroom punch-ups than boxing. Indeed, I was doing press-ups four days before the operation!

I was fortunate enough to have friends in the right places to help me in my hour of need but I believe these programmes are available on many websites and magazines. Ultimately, I did not need to use a walking frame at all. I dallied with double crutches for twenty-four hours to appease the hospital's physio (too much like knitting needles!) and went on thereafter to a single walking stick.

On Day Two, two burly hospital porters came to my bedside with a mobile bed, with instructions to take me down for a check-up MRI. I refused to take advantage of the bed and stated that I was going to walk to the elevator and down to the X-ray area. They were thus obliged to follow me, dutifully pushing the empty bed back down to the lower ground floor.

Indeed, to quote Dr Goleman's study, 'Those women who [sought mindset help] with other medical care needed less physical therapy to walk again and had fewer rehospitalizations over the three months after their return home.'

The wonderful thing about a hip operation is that you know when it is going to happen and, therefore, you can plan/prepare around it.

The outcome: less than three weeks after the operation, I walked into Mr Radford's room, brandishing my now-redundant walking stick. It was a pleasure to watch this eminent surgeon's jaw drop in amazement. Whilst most patients usually require a minimum of six to eight weeks to be discharged, Mr Radford was happy to discharge me there and then.

Having got to the stage of walking unaided, it still took another three weeks for the new hip and muscle to 'gel' together (my term!). Thus, I still had to sit at a ninety-degree angle and carry my crutch when going out – if only to alert passers-by not to collide with me. When possible, I made use of preferential seating on the London buses.

Being hands-free again gave me a sense of freedom and empowerment that cannot be described adequately. Sadly, my stilettos remained on hold till the full six-week total recovery period. You might say my high heels remained the carrot at the end of my walking stick! A small price to pay for what was ultimately the return to normality.

A word of caution: 'Change doesn't happen overnight; success is the sum of small efforts repeated day in and day out. If we make the effort, we will get better. If we don't, we won't'.[14]

---

14   Marshall Goldsmith, p. 139.

Sometimes things happen unexpectedly and we need a mindset of resilience to manage that. Some people boast (and this is something I hate) that they could see something happening, so they decided to do this or that. However, we cannot always know. As Bruce Feiler puts it, 'A hallmark of our time is that life is not predictable. It does not unfold in passages, stages, phases, or cycles. It is nonlinear.'[15]

Life presents what Feiler calls 'disruptors'. For me, the biggest disruptor was abandoning my entrepreneurial and business goals (at that time, taking advantage of EU tax breaks to erect solar parks on agricultural land in Italy) and becoming the sole carer for my ailing parents.

I always had a choice about taking on their care, but I was an only child and felt it was my duty. The caring lasted nine years and ended up virtually destroying me and certainly annihilating my identity (for too long...). In the same way that their exaggerated demands and expectations fashioned me into becoming a more resilient person, this period in my life ultimately led me to experiment with mentoring and, ultimately, coaching and, thereby, my present business (and, you might even say, this very book...).

To put things differently, whilst we always have a choice, events can still have a significant impact on our lives. In my case, if I hadn't quit my business venture in solar parks, I might not have delved into mentoring and then I would not have

---

15   Bruce Feiler, *Life is in The Transitions* (Penguin Press, 2020), p. 47.

progressed into coaching. However, in no way could I claim, 'I saw this and then that and decided to ...' In truth, in my forty-five-plus years in business, I have only taken two career-changing decisions:

► Moving from academia to corporate
► Adopting coaching as my next venture

The rest was, to some extent, going with the flow.

As Feiler puts it, 'We need to make the most of our transitions.'[16] In other words, the changes do not happen in one fell swoop. He goes on to elaborate on the different stages you might go through to effect that change. If you do not believe that change takes place in steps, then just go back to nature and consider the humble chrysalis that ultimately becomes a butterfly.

To further reinforce this statement, I quote Nicola Bunting: 'The best way to negotiate the rapids of change is to step up and into them... It means allowing your journey to start with an ending, accepting that ending... and giving yourself permission to explore and tolerate not knowing where you're going, while you get more clarity on where you really *want* to go.'[17]

This beautiful quote is wonderfully illustrated by Mahatma Gandhi's physical, cultural and emotional journey. A journey

---

16   Feiler, p. 157.
17   Nicola Bunting, p. 218.

that involved him adopting Western (and South African) mores, including food, dress and ways of living, until he was some 40 years of age (by my count) when he was able to formulate his own doctrine.

A recurring theme in this book is how we perceive events. As Dr C. S. Dweck states, '...you do not get a growth mindset by proclamation. You move toward it by taking a journey'.[18] What I call STEPS.

Lady Hale, the former president of the Supreme Court, has been honest enough to talk about her early feelings as an imposter which took her several decades to overcome. From being the only girl to have passed the 11-plus exam, right up to the moment she announced the judgment of the Supreme Court in September 2019 that brought her worldwide attention.[19]

It was also somewhere during this time that she developed the habit, suggested by her late husband, the lawyer Julien Farrand, of wearing the irreverent animal brooches that have become her trademark.

If you ever needed an example of doing things in small steps, this is the best! Even if it means taking two steps forward and one step back '...it can allow a richer, more grounded

---

18   Dweck, p. 217.

19   Harper's Bazaar interview, Nov 2021 quoting exerts from her book *The Spider Woman* (Penguin, 2021).

redefinition of our working identity to emerge'.[20] Herminia Ibarra goes on to illustrate the point with a case study of a woman she calls Susan Fontaine,[21] who accepted the first job to come her way only to quit two weeks later.

It was only after Susan took time off to reassess her values and what was important to her that she came to understand the type of work she should be undertaking. By taking small steps, she was able to create what Karl E. Weick calls 'small wins'.[22] Ultimately, it took Susan two years to find the solution, but during those two years, she made new contacts, discovered that freelancing suited her and identified a new sector to apply her marketing skills in: charity.

Career change can also involve changing your 'shifting connections'.[23] For instance, in writing this book, I made innumerable contacts around the specialist subjects I touch upon.

---

20 Herminia Ibarra, *Working Identity* (Harvard Business Press, 2003), p. 67-68.

21 Ibarra, pp. 68-72.

22 Karl E. Weick, *Small Wins: 'Reflecting the Scale of Social Problems'*, *American Psychologist 39, no 1* (January 1984): pp. 40-49.

23 Ibarra, p. 122.

ASK YOURSELF:

Are there any negative experiences in your professional life from which you can learn a lesson?

List any negative thoughts attached to those experiences here.

How can you look at them differently?

CHAPTER 3

HOW I LEARNT TO NEVER GIVE UP

During my career, I worked for one of the biggest bullies in the world: Robert Maxwell. If you do not know who this man was, think of Rupert Murdoch (his arch rival), Donald Trump or Lord Sugar, in terms of corporate stature. Maxwell (also known as RM or 'Captain Bob') had an empire that included British Printing Corporation, Mirror Group Newspapers, and Macmillan Publishers, among other publishing companies. He was also a major shareholder in MTV Europe.

As you will have seen in the last chapter's video, my first interview with him was aired on BBC2's *Money Programme* in 1987. Does this sound like *The Apprentice*? Too right! In fact, not only was this the first reality show in history, but it was also the precursor to *The Apprentice*, but for real! In the course of the programme,[24] you will see how Maxwell (playing to the camera) starts talking to me in French (he was an excellent linguist). I answer his questions and then comment, '*Vous avez un excellent accent*' (you have a great French accent), which gives him the opportunity to preen all the more.

---

24 https://www.youtube.com/watch?v=f6k5i2AfPHA

This retort came from a habitual strategy of mine to (re)gain control of a situation or, if you prefer, to turn the tables. And, boy, did I have to do that with him and his authoritarian attitude towards employees! I was greatly helped, though, in that I was not an alpha male in his jungle so I was not perceived as a threat.

I wish to dwell a bit here on my Maxwell 'experience' as it illustrates four important points, which I have used in my career:

1. Do not be afraid to be a woman in a man's world.

2. Fight for what you want.

3. Everything is not what it appears to be; when you discover this, deal with the situation and fight again!

4. Step out of the situation and realise that the boss is only looking to 'enhance their own feelings of power, competence and value at the subordinate's expense'.[25]

So, picture this: we are in the summer of 1987. The headhunter has taken me through all the hurdles of various interviews and I am offered the job. I am expected to visit Maxwell and accept the position in front of the camera. However, there is no contract; nothing at all in writing regarding my new role as Head of the European Business Channel, which he was looking to launch. I put my foot down (off camera, clearly!)

---

25   Quoted in Dweck, p. 123 from Harvey Hornstein, *Brutal Bosses.*

and stated that there was no way I was going to appear on nationwide television, still gainfully employed, without a contract. Needless to say, I got that written contract!

Thus, I became the Chief Executive of this new channel at a salary of £75,000 a year (the equivalent of £225,000 today). Or maybe not... Three months after my appointment, I presented myself to *The Daily Mirror* building and was warmly greeted by the receptionist.

All was not what it appeared to be. The lovely receptionist instructed me to take the lift to the fourth floor and ask for Peter Laister, who was a director of Maxwell's interests in television. Peter, who had been the chairman of Thorn and then Thorn EMI, was always the gentleman and invited me into his office. This first meeting served to slowly unveil the 'truth' behind my appointment: there was no European Business Channel. I did not have an office, I did not have a desk, I did not have a phone.

In other words, I had been hired at a fabulous salary for a job that did not exist! To say that the earth fell from under my feet would be an understatement. The whole thing behind my appointment was a charade or, at the very least, a fantasy in the mind of the mighty Maxwell. I had left a great job that had enabled me to travel around Europe in style, dealing with CEOs, partners at law and accountancy firms – for what?

This is where the primeval instinct of Fight, Fright or Flight comes in. Imagine my utter amazement; was it possible that, after being interviewed on television, chosen for the job and interviewed by the press, the project did not exist? What should I do? Go back to my old job, cap in hand, full of humility? Or stay and find a 'real' job?

Finally, emboldened by my survival instinct, I started exploring what was going on in the Maxwell empire, outside of the Mirror Group newspapers. Fortunately, in my wanderings around the building searching for a desk/phone/chair (and it was going to be sorting *myself* out – no one was going to do that for me) I met up with two lovely guys, Jonathan and Jeff, who explained to me how satellite transmission worked. You have to remember that satellite TV was a new industry in the late eighties, the most illustrious example being British Satellite Television, which later became BSkyB in 1990 (now Sky).

In the course of these various exchanges, I came across a joint venture called Pergamon GED – involving Maxwell Communications, China's Central Television and CITIC (the PRC's investment company), and a US company called GED. The concept behind this company was to provide educational programmes to the people of China, sponsored (i.e. paid for) by enterprises doing business in that country. The project was not going well at all and I felt that my previous experience in publishing/advertising could help me turn it around. The company was being run by a senior TV executive who, in my opinion, was in the wrong job; someone with an understanding of sponsorship was required.

I communicated my ideas to Peter and two of Maxwell's sons, Kevin and Ian, who passed them on to the man himself. Anyhow, to cut a long story short...after a brief meeting with Maxwell (he had a very short attention span), I was appointed as the new Chief Executive of Pergamon GED – three months after coming on board for a job that did not exist. So, I had at least secured myself a job – and a lifeline...

Peter Laister also suggested that I look into a company they were checking out; it made video-conferencing equipment for use in company offices. The company also had a suite in the Intercontinental Hotel at Hyde Park Corner. This room could be let by the hour and used to communicate with other similar suites around the world.

I saw the potential of this new technology which enabled executives to meet with their counterparts around the world without leaving the comfort of their office. Video conferencing was the precursor of Skype, Zoom and other similar services of today, but it was very expensive and required some serious pieces of furniture the size of a tallboy, not to mention some bespoke cabling at both ends.

The company was pitching its service at the level of the IT manager. I felt it stood better chances of success if the CEO of the company was targeted. Firstly, because it was a very expensive purchase for which there was no budget; secondly, because many employers saw travel as a perk in those days, recommending such a new service could make the proposal unpopular; and, thirdly, once the purchase was authorised by the CEO, it did not have to be justified.

Eventually, we bought the company and renamed it Maxwell Satellite Communications. It was understood that this new entity would come under my responsibility, but I had no title to reflect this. I felt this was important, not only for internal purposes but also for dealings with the 'outside world'. The renamed company already had a managing director (from the original set-up). I, therefore, suggested that I should be appointed as Chief Executive.

This request fell on deaf ears (those of Peter Laister, Kevin and Ian Maxwell), as the ultimate decision lay with Robert Maxwell. Never one to give up, I seized the moment when Kevin and I happened to share a lift one day. Talk about 'The Elevator Pitch'. Suffice to say that I was successful.

A positive mindset is a key feature, as is expressed by James Reed (Chairman of the Reed Group). It even supersedes a skill set! Resilience, positivity and global awareness will make you stand out. Do not give up – keep on going!

Today, thanks to the pandemic, many people are working from home. This presents a challenge. Zoom might have allowed you to wear pyjama bottoms with a nice shirt; your shaving/make-up habits might have become more 'relaxed'... (and we will not talk about footwear!). Your mindset has probably also taken a knock for lack of stimulus. So what do you do to get your mind working again?

1. In the words of the military, Perfect Preparation Prevents Piss Poor Performance – or, translated into today's language, garner as much information as you can from the web; for instance. If you are preparing for an interview, consult sites like Glassdoor, where you can read employees' views of the potential employer; armed with this data, consider the questions you are going to ask.

2. Use old-fashioned networking, or 'connecting', as I prefer to say. Good conversations stimulate the brain and will spur you to go forth.

3. Rehearsing for the interview plays an even more important part than it did in the pre-COVID days. After all, it has been a long time since you have 'presented' yourself as a worthy candidate. To put it more bluntly, you are out of practice.

4. Surround yourself with positive people. If you do have a chum or even a career coach like me, you may even apply for jobs you are not so keen on, just to get into the 'swing of things' again.

5. Do not be put off by rejection. If you are like me, you may not fit neatly into a box but consider what transferable skills you have. When applying for my first job, I persisted regardless of the numerous turn-downs, and finally got a job working for an import-export company. They felt it would be quicker to

teach a linguist the ins and outs of trading, rather than hiring a trader who could not speak several languages. What saved me was the fact that I spoke three languages: French, English and Italian.

My linguistic skills then led me to my second job working for a barter company owned by Bowater/Ralli.

My big break came in the early eighties with the American publishing house, Institutional Investor, where I stayed for seven years, dealing only with partners at law/accountancy firms, heads of international banks, and senior corporate executives throughout Europe and the Middle East.

I was then headhunted in 1987 to join the Maxwell empire and subsequently became the first European Business Development Director for the NASDAQ stock market. When NASDAQ changed its focus from being client-facing to being trader-centric, I was made redundant and started a business in solar energy – identifying agricultural land in Italy that could be converted into solar parks.

So, you see, I have been in trading, publishing, telecom, finance and energy for over twenty years. Sadly, this desire to keep on going came to a halt when, in the early 2000s, I dropped the solar business to become a carer; first for my mother, then my father and, to some extent, my suicidal husband. As a carer, I was on call 24 hours a day, 365 days a year, and was unable to take up any paid work, but I kept up my interest in people by taking up mentoring whenever possible.

Now, with hindsight, I can see that these nine years of caring also allowed me to reflect on my career thus far. I had to recognise that my appeal as a corporate employee was gone. Sylvia Ann Hewlett and Carolyn Buck Luce discuss this at length.[26] More often than not, women step away from work to look after their children; others, like myself, do so to care for their elderly parents. Hewlett and Black refer to us returners as 'Lost on Re-entry'[27] and call for companies to change their views and stop marginalising female work-returners. They quote the accountancy firm, Ernst & Young, as an example to follow, but such an option did not even exist at the time. The only possibility for me was to be self-employed, but doing what?

I was not going to give up. I reflected on my life and career and recognised that, as a corporate executive, I had already been coaching staff in facing change. I decided to combine my academic skills with my corporate experience by going on a coaching course and setting myself up (12 years ago now) as a Coach/Mentor and Business Strategist.

Some three years after Alastair's eventual suicide[28] (several years after his trip to Scotland), I went online and discovered

---

26　'Off-Ramps and On-Ramps', HBR's 10 Must Reads *On Women and Leadership*, 2019.

27　Sylvia Ann Hewlett and Carolyn Buck Luce, p. 162.

28　I have related this story in the *Metro* and am happy to say it has prevented at least two people from taking their lives, as well as helping relatives of those who have attempted suicide.

the world of internet dating and the challenges it poses. Thus, a new branch of my coaching business came into effect: Dr Catherine, Dating Guru® – helping men and women over the age of fifty to have a safe and fun journey looking for their new partner online. At an age when most people would retire, I had started a new venture and was loving it!

Unfortunately, this new venture did not take off, as it coincided with the COVID lockdown. So, once more, at an age when most of my contemporaries retire, I relaunched my executive coaching services under a new brand name: www. drcatherinecoaching.com.

If you look closely at the Dr Catherine Coaching logo, you will see the triangle, which represents the three sides to my career (academic, corporate and coaching) over the letter 'i' in my name:

And with the re-branding has come a re-definition of my four core coaching services:

- ► Career Change
- ► Executive Coaching
- ► Getting a Promotion
- ► Personal Development

In the same spirit that I would be sent to school with a high temperature and expected to come out with the top results,[29] I have rarely allowed myself to cancel existing appointments.

---

29   As related in Chapter 2.

Only recently, whilst being interviewed by Anita Goyal for her podcast, Light Up Your Fire, I revealed that I had just come out of an eight-day stay in the hospital, with a double hip fracture and was undergoing a high dose of morphine administered through a patch to my arm. Anita was stunned...

'The right mindset, combined with perseverance and dedication, can create [new opportunities], regardless of age.'[30] This is another way of saying, 'Do not give up.' In a recent blog, Ashley Bishop poses the question as to whether your mindset is sabotaging your health.[31]

As if to illustrate the point even further, I have just been approached by an entrepreneur, Joe, to chair his latest venture in the realm of sports. I accepted without hesitation, even though it means restructuring my business and, to some extent, my life.

Why this drive, you might ask? The main reason is that I just *cannot* retire. Were I to give up 'working', I would fall apart and die.

When I say, 'Keep on going', I do not mean 'Keep on doing the same thing'. As Einstein expressed it, a sure sign of madness is doing the same thing over and over again and expecting a different result.

---

30 Som Bathla, *Mindset Makeover* (Amazon, 2021), p. 31.

31 https://www.ashleybishop.co.uk/is-your-mindset-sabotaging-your-health.

I am talking about not giving up at the sign of adversity. There is no question: the COVID outbreak and ensuing lockdown have affected everyone. In my case, as a coach, it virtually annihilated my business. Coaching is about creating a safe environment, in which the client finds a space to think, reflect and ponder. Unfortunately, this is difficult to achieve when your Zoom meeting can be overheard by other parties in your household.

At the same time, I am not a person who can stay at home twiddling her thumbs. A recent survey conducted by the University of Pennsylvania and UCLA covered 21,700 people between 2012 and 2013. The outcome was that, unsurprisingly, higher levels of free time were significantly associated with greater well-being. More interesting, though, was the revelation that excess leisure had the opposite effect. In other words, too much time on your hands can lead to stress. A healthy dose of activity can enhance your performance and your health.

Faced with the 'challenge' of not being able to exercise my coaching skills (note, dear Reader: not 'problem' or 'obstacle', but 'challenge' – keeping positive throughout!), I was inspired by one of my mentees (and now friend after 10 years!), the delightful Federico, to take on tutoring English as a second language.

Armed with a PhD in Comparative Literature, I duly applied to a site that pairs students up with a tutor. My profile listed Business English as my principal offering. After all, I had been a corporate executive and well prepared to teach the lingo to aspiring executives. Once again, I came to realise I had transferrable skills.

Within no time, my diary was filled with lessons with delightful people from all over the world: Russia, Denmark, France, Italy, Holland, Ukraine, Hong Kong, etc. Often, I could not stop myself from combining English tutoring with my coaching techniques.

For instance, a very bright young French university graduate from one of the top French universities was looking to apply for an interim placement to complement his education. I am pleased to say that, after some role-playing, he obtained a temporary post with Ernst & Young and, subsequently, was offered a full-time position.

Another student was an IT expert from Hong Kong who wished to rid himself of his 'Chinese accent' (his term, not mine). As it turns out, he also needed a lot more tools to assimilate into a British environment: soft skills, such as engaging with his colleagues and even his yoga classmates. A fast-learning and incredibly diligent student, he recorded our sessions and put my suggestions into practice. He learnt to ask for advice. He changed his habits; when coming across a fellow gym member bearing a plaster cast on her arm, he stopped to enquire what had happened to her. In the past, he would have just carried on without engaging into a conversation. He had learnt how to 'chat' and not limit his conversation to business issues. He is now applying this new skill daily in his exchanges with colleagues. You might well say this is not earth-shattering and that it's nothing novel. But, the point is, it is novel to him and it is helping him break down barriers.

Fate would have it that two current coaching assignments have also led me to adopt the role of a Business Strategist (which, in my normal self-deprecating manner, I refer to as a BullShi**er). My two clients could not be more different; one is the Joe mentioned above who is looking to start a sports venture; the other is an NHS GP wanting to set up a private specialist service. It is, however, such a natural fit to my past corporate experience and coaching abilities, that I am surprised I had not thought of it before and can quite see it might take over my other activities.

One thing is for sure: I will give these two ventures my very best advice and viewpoint. Just watch this space.

The last point I'd like to mention about the importance of keeping going has to do with the people around you. Like it or not, we are social animals and, just as our surroundings affect us, so too do our friends. They have a great impact on our mindset.

Surround yourself with positive people. Doom mongers and bullies will bring you down into their sad little world.

Tony Robbins says, 'Who you spend time with is who you become!' and that you should surround yourself with people with 'higher standards'. I would rather say (sorry Mr Robins!), surround yourself with people with a fresh, inquisitive mindset. For me, this is very often younger people as they are more likely to have a growth mindset.

In the words of the supermodel Giselle Bündchen, 'If I had totally believed the bullies in my school, or the people in the fashion industry who criticised my appearance, my self-doubt would have paralysed me.'[32]

Stay upbeat and, not only will people gravitate towards you, but you will refresh your dynamism and enthusiasm. Something is fascinating about how positive energy attracts people; it is like an invisible magnet. I am told that I exude a lot of this type of vibe and must admit that there are times when I do seem to attract fellow delegates or attendees to come and talk to me.

When you are in negative company, remember that you always have a choice and that it can involve reframing the problem – for which you need a constructive mindset.

If you do not believe me, consider this statement from Ant Middleton: 'I know what I need to be positive. I need positive values, a positive mindset and positive people around me...If you hang around with negative people, then you shouldn't be surprised if you end up behaving negatively yourself.'[33]

Enjoy friends' positivity and their 'newness'. 'You'll be bouncing off each other rather than sucking away each other's will to

---

32   Bündchen, p. 135.

33   Ant Middleton, *Zero Negativity* (Harper Collins, 2021), p. 78.

live',[34] comments Ashley Bishop. Learn from them by seeing things from their perspective and, in return, share your take on certain situations. This mutual exchange can enrich both your lives.

In other instances, these positive people may be your family. Many businesswomen relate how their professional endeavours could not have happened without a supportive spouse.

ASK YOURSELF:

Have you been in a situation where you did not have work and undertook a 'lesser' assignment from which other benefits were reaped? Elaborate here.

How supportive are your friends and family?

34   See [7.]

CHAPTER 4

IMPOSTER SYNDROME – FEELINGS ARE NOT FACTS

Imposter syndrome is a collection of feelings of inadequacy, despite evidence of success. The psychotherapist Owen O'Kane argues that anyone can suffer from this condition and that it '...can often be exacerbated by feelings that success and perfection are linked'.[35]

Of all the definitions of imposter syndrome, one of my favourites is by Hibberd: 'Imposter syndrome normally occurs when there is a tension between two views – yours and what you believe others expect of you.[36] Because you believe yourself to be a phoney, any good feelings around your success are short-lived.'[37]

---

35   Owen O'Kane, https://blog.asana.com/2021/04/overcome-imposter-syndrome/?mkt_tok=Nzg0LVhaRC01ODIAAAF_jQX-Gx71NPJ00xGl0raE89Ib1ldD_TArTVuDX_k-e1OyKdNvMANJ5M57vYJz RDQhsylULUhasMUCp0hvbtz4WcTwBO3KFcm0h1jYiZX5CQ#close

36   Hibberd, p.38.

37   Valerie Young Ed.D., *The Secret Thoughts of Successful Women* (Crown Business, 2011), p.73

Or, as Valerie Young puts it, 'You are already successful. You just don't own it.'[38]

Imposter syndrome has several easily recognisable signs. It comes with thinking:

- ► You are a fraud.

- ► You have only got to where you are by sheer luck.

- ► You have been clever at hiding your failures and stand the risk of being 'found out'.

- ► The 'truth' (your perception of yourself as a hoax) is bound to come out soon.

- ► If you put yourself forward for that job, everyone will see that 'truth'.

Here are some of the ways you'd behave:

- ► You procrastinate and put off doing tasks because you believe they will reveal your weaknesses.

- ► You overwork in an effort to cover your 'mistakes'.

- ► You focus on your mistakes.

- ► You are fearful of speaking up.

---

38   Valerie Young, p.1.

► You have a fear of failure.

► You attribute your success to luck. 'Success is simply a matter of luck. Ask any failure.' (Earl Nightingale)

Thankfully, imposter syndrome can be overcome:

► Recognise that success is NOT perfection.

► Talk about your past in the third person.

► Start liking yourself.

► Remember the wise words of Eleanor Roosevelt: 'No one can make you feel inferior without your consent.'

► Recognise that what is holding you back are FEELINGS and FEELINGS are not FACTS! In the words of Danielle Dobson, 'Your thinking determines your reality.'[39]

► Talk about your doubts with a friend, colleague, or coach.

► Take five minutes to write down what success means to you. Put another way, what are you not willing to sacrifice to have money, status, and power?

My own story is not free of this pervasive syndrome. As in most life episodes, there is a sub-text to my acceptance of the job in Maxwell's media empire. I had a very good job at

---

39   Danielle Dobson, *Code Conversation, 2020*, p. 167.

the time – working for Institutional Investor as their European Head of Conferences. I travelled in style and dealt directly (and only) with the top decision-makers. It was during one of those conferences, at the Villa d'Este in Como, that I met one of the loves of my life: Christopher Harding (later Sir Christopher Harding).

The conference was an event for the CEOs of major European companies and their spouses. Christopher was there representing Hanson Trust, at the time, one of the world's largest companies with annual profits of more than £1.5 billion and a strategy of growth through acquisition. Christopher was MD of Hanson Transport (a key founding company in the Hanson Empire) and, shortly afterwards, became the newly appointed CEO of British Nuclear Fuels plc.

Christopher was divorced and I fell head-over-heels in love with this handsome executive. Whilst I had been through the initial interview with the head-hunter 'without deviation, or hesitation' (to paraphrase Radio 4's *Just a Minute*), I started to stumble and wondered whether I was up to the position being offered to me by Robert Maxwell.

I had the security of a job I truly enjoyed (and in which I was flourishing). Four dialogues were going on in my head:

- ► Why leave?
- ► Better the devil you know
- ► On the other hand, this is a great opportunity
- ► Could I do the job?

It was probably the first time in my life that I asked myself whether I should carry on.

Or, in the words of Valerie Young, 'What have you got to gain by giving up? What price are you paying for this? What would you miss?'[40] At the time, my job at Institutional Investor took me on a plane three or four times a month to a European city. In those days (the eighties), business travel was still done in style. All the more so, as Institutional Investor owned a magazine that set up barter arrangements with airlines and hotel chains (advertising spots paid for in equivalent US dollars for airline seats or hotel rooms). This was a perfectly legitimate transaction that suited all parties.

Furthermore, I was on a professional high at the time; the eighties marked the de-nationalisation of most Spanish institutions and it was a case of being in the right place at the right time. It resulted in my taking the likes of Telefonica (then, Compania Telefonica), a couple of the country's utility companies, banks and even the Madrid Stock Exchange itself, to make presentations. I did so under my employer's banner in Tokyo, New York and London, in front of the relevant country's institutional investors.

In her book, *Lean In*, Sandberg relates the story of Google, which created a system whereby 'engineers nominate themselves for promotions [and] the company found that men nominated themselves more quickly than women'.

---

40   V. Young, p. 87.

When the management 'shared the data openly with the female employees, [...] women's self-nomination rates rose significantly, reaching roughly the same rates as men'.[41]

Christopher encouraged me to go ahead and helped me dispel this imposter syndrome. The phenomenon is not unique to women but it is unquestionably a recurring trait in female executives. Whereas a male may go forth and worry about things later, women tend to worry more about the detail and question themselves concerning their ability to 'do the job'. In her book *The Authority Gap*, Mary Ann Sieghart[42] interviews the likes of Baroness Hale, former president of the UK Supreme Court (the most senior judge in the land), and Christine Lagarde, who both admit to having experienced those moments of self-doubt.

According to Tara Halliday, 70 per cent of high-achievers are affected by imposter syndrome at some point in their lives. Gill Whitty-Collins prefers to call imposter syndrome, *the perfectionist syndrome*.[43]

I will be eternally grateful to Christopher for encouraging me to 'go for it'. After that, it was up to me... But he set the seed for me to proceed regardless.

Sadly, my relationship with him did not last more than three years. However, when Christopher was knighted, he wrote me

---

41   Sandberg, *Lean In*, Chapter 10, p. 149.
42   Mary Ann Sieghart, *The Authority Gap* (Penguin, 2021), pp. 84-85.
43   Gill Whitty Collins.

a long hand-written letter in his customary green ink saying that much of his success was due to me. In his missive, he recognised that he had been severely knocked by the failure of his first marriage and that I had helped him regain his self-esteem and take on the professional challenges his new role as CEO of British Nuclear Fuels had thrown at him. Under the veneer of a knighthood and a job title of chief executive, he was, after all, a human being with weaknesses and uncertainties.

A further three or more years later, he died prematurely from an aneurism.

His support made me rethink my evaluation of myself. Since then, I have studied coaching and have realised that I too (intermittently) suffer from imposter syndrome. I go from one pole to the other. I can move from being the 'court jester', full of braggadocio and energy, to being quiet, reflective,[44] with a tendency to display the signs listed above.

There have been times when I have been paralysed by this feeling of being either 'fake' or very 'lucky'. I would see a request from a journalist to talk to a specialist in (say) re-careering (which is one of my specialisations) and fail to volunteer because I did not think I had anything to contribute. *Best to keep a low profile and not make a fool of myself.*

In the same way, I have procrastinated for years to write this book. I now happily respond to journalists' requests

---

44   Dr Jessamy Hibberd, *The Imposter Cure* (Aster 2019), p. 13.

for editorial content. How did I achieve this (note the word 'achieve', for it IS an accomplishment)? After all, I had stood up to the Maxwells of this world, met with Heads of State, Captains of Industry, and yet, for a while, would turn down speaking (and writing) opportunities.

I started by looking back at what had happened to me in the last fifteen or more years. I not only looked back but also started to analyse how my life had been of late.

I had given up my career, and my life, to become my parents' carer for those nine excruciating years. I had come out of that very taxing time wondering who I was. The problem is that once you allow self-doubt to come in, it can take hold. That self-doubt persisted, hidden under a veil of confident 'bravura'. What I had to do is recognise that both the bravura and my humour were a mask to cover my insecurity.

What helped was that I joined the worldwide networking organisation, BNI. My membership involved my making a sixty-second long presentation of my business – week in, week out. Additionally, on a rotation basis, I would make a ten-minute speech. Ultimately, I took on additional roles in leadership which required further public interventions. The old Catherine was slowly coming back!

I am not saying that BNI is the sole key to overcoming imposter syndrome; there are plenty of other associations, such as Toastmasters, which can provide the same result. It is just the one that I came across and the one that helped me make this transition back to the 'old me'. To refer back to the quote from Hibberd, I managed, over time, to kill the 'tension between two views – yours and what you believe others expect of you'.

I also was able to recognise that failing was not the end of the world. In the words of Churchill, 'Success is not final, failure is not fatal: it is the courage to continue that counts.' Mistakes and failure can make you more resilient.[45]

Imposter syndrome is best diffused by self-acceptance and, in particular, the realisation that you are as entitled to success as the person next to you. However, to get there, you need to change your mindset and I have since discovered the amazing WIND Formula summarised by Bathla.[46]

W.I.N.D. stands for:

- ► W – Witness negative thoughts and detach yourself from these situations
- ► I – Interdict negative thoughts
- ► N – Nurture your mind with positive affirmations
- ► D – Drive to your new mental state with zeal

Of course, one of the many reasons for imposter syndrome is fear of failure. It will not surprise you, therefore, that one of the key books I recommend to young entrepreneurs is Susan Jeffers, *Feel the Fear and Do It Anyway.*[47]

---

45   Quoted in Hibberd, p. 170 *passim*.

46   Bathla, pp. 79 *passim*.

47   Podcast.

I have learnt to be kinder to myself and to forgive myself for my (perceived) shortcomings. I have also learnt to accept the support of my friends.[48]

If you feel you are an imposter, take heart from Bertrand Russell: 'The whole problem with the world is that fools and fanatics are always so certain of themselves, and wiser people are full of doubts.'

As Clifton relates, no matter how good you are at what you do, it is very difficult to coach yourself. And it is specifically difficult to coach yourself out of imposter syndrome, so take advantage of what is available to join – within or outside your workplace.

ASK YOURSELF:

Do you think you suffer from imposter syndrome?

What are you going to do to change that?

---

48   This is further endorsed by Daniel Goleman, p. 158 *passim.*

CHAPTER 5

LIMITING BELIEFS

We touched earlier on how your upbringing/childhood can impact your behaviour. The same impact can be attributed to limiting beliefs.

The dictionary defines limiting beliefs as 'those [beliefs] which constrain us in some way. Just by believing them, we do not think, do or say the things that they inhibit. And in doing so we impoverish our lives. Limiting beliefs are often about ourselves and our self-identity.'

I started with the belief that I did not need anyone around me; I could do it by myself. The solitude of research for my PhD suited me fine as I was not being distracted by anything or anybody. I just ploughed on and got on with it.

Mercifully, the corporate world taught me I am not an island. To achieve corporate goals, work had to be undertaken in unison with my colleagues and my staff. I also discovered the power of friendship.

As Max Mason puts it, 'beliefs create reality.'[49] But they do not create the truth.

---

49   Max Mason, *Stop Doubting Yourself* (Amazon, 2021) p. 21.

The highly esteemed Dr Jessamy Hibberd puts it another way; '...as a child, it's impossible to know that this is one person's view and that this person may not be a good judge, and so you internalize what they say as the truth.'[50]

For instance, my parents were not good at complimenting my academic, personal or professional successes. Picture this: I am aged fifty or so and am visiting my parents with a girlfriend, Jane, with whom I was going out for lunch. On the way, we pop into the parental home to check on the folks and then, over a glass of wine (my parents were very good hosts), René suddenly declares, 'Jane, you are such a lovely lady. How can you possibly be friends with Catherine?'

At the time I had given up my career and my business to care for both him and Anne-Marie.

When we left the house, Jane asked me, 'How can you put up with that sort of behaviour?' The truth is I was inured to it and still did not know how to respond.

Slowly, slowly, I learnt how to distance myself from my authoritarian parents. Part of the distancing was calling them by their first name; they were no longer 'Maman' and 'Papa' but they were 'Anne-Marie' and 'René'. In terms of Transactional Analysis, I had ceased to be a child and had escalated myself to being an adult.

---

50   Dr Jessamy Hibberd, *The Imposter Cure*, (Aster 2019), p. 63.

Ironically, they never understood what I was doing by addressing them differently. One day, Anne-Marie explained that 'It's a trendy thing.' Fine. I was not bothered by that. I was on my journey towards asserting myself.

The lesson from this is that you can come across as having *gravitas,* but you are still often a child in some of your relationships with others. What you need to do is to identify those limiting beliefs and replace them; recognising that:

- ► Past failures do not define your future
- ► You can handle anything that happens
- ► You can learn from past failures
- ► Overcoming obstacles is proof of success
- ► If something does not work, try something else[51]
- ► You can always reframe your beliefs

'You are old,' said the youth, 'as I mentioned before,
And have grown most uncommonly fat;
Yet you turned a back-somersault in at the door
Pray, what is the reason of that?'[52]

This delightful poem is a perfect illustration of limiting beliefs; the youth is expressing his (unfounded) assumption that fat, old people are not agile.

The perception of women in business is equally subject to limiting beliefs.

---

51   Mason, *Stop Doubting Yourself* p. 78 *passim.*
52   Lewis Carroll, Father William.

The truth of the matter is that we all carry an unconscious belief (I would even dare to say unconscious bias) that women are not meant to be executives. If only I had a pound for every time someone assumed during my tenure at Maxwell's that I was his secretary! It wasn't just men, either!

Similarly, a woman's behaviour is also subject to different interpretations: assertive, arrogant, resilient, impertinent, bully.[53]

Consider the different adjectives attributed to men versus women for the same behaviour and language:

Men	Women
Commanding	Bossy
Assertive	Bitch
Persistent	Pushy
Decisive	Impulsive
Blowing off steam	Hysterical
Weighing his options	Can't make up her mind
Rational	Emotional

---

53   Sieghart in her Chapter 11 on *Women in Politics*.

Put otherwise, in the words of Tomas Chamorro-Premuzic, 'When a woman does seem as confident as, or more confident than men, we are put off by her because high confidence does not fit our gender stereotypes.'[54]

My question, though, is would they make the same judgement if a man used the same language in his office environment?

As quoted by Helgesen/Goldsmith, Sheryl Sandberg and Adam Grant wrote in the NY Times, 'women who speak assertively are far more likely than men to be viewed negatively at work.' The real problem, they concluded, seems to be speaking while female.[55] A study carried out at Harvard Business School concluded that 'success and likeability are positively correlated for men and negatively correlated for women'.[56] This is reiterated by Premuzic: 'Women are punished for displaying many traits regarded as central to leadership emergence. Ambition, risk-taking, assertiveness, and other similar traits are frowned on in women because they are stereotypically masculine. And yet, when a woman fails to display such traits – meaning she behaves in traditionally feminine ways – she is easily dismissed for not being leader-like... Consequently,

---

54   Tomas Charmirri-Premuzic, *Why Do so Many Incompetent Men Become Leaders? (and How to Fix It)*. p. 31.

55   *How Women Rise*, p. 153.

56   Quoted by Sheryl Sandberg, in *Lean In* (WH Allen, 2015), Chapter 3, p. 40.

women need to be more qualified than men do to compete with men for the same leadership roles.'[57]

Whilst on the subject of talking, voice plays an important part as well. There is no better example of this than Margaret Thatcher, Britain's first female prime minister who underwent elocution lessons to lower her voice. Sieghart dedicates a full chapter to the way females express themselves versus their male counterparts.[58] Previously, Mary Beard relates, 'As one ancient scientific treatise explicitly put it, a low-pitched voice indicated courage, a high-pitched voice cowardice.'[59] She contends that the banning of the female voice goes back to Ancient Greece and continues to say, 'It is not what you say that prompts [insults], it's simply the fact that you're saying it.'[60]

What is rarely mentioned in books, though, is that, in addition to the voice, the content is also important. To use one of my favourite American acronyms: KISS – Keep It Short and Simple.[61]

---

57   Premuzic, p. 127-8.

58   Sieghart, *Conversation Manspreading*, Chapter 6.

59   Mary Beard, *Women & Power*, (Profile Books, 2017) p. 19.

60   Mary Beard, p. 36-7.

61   Lois P Frankel touches on this, p. 223-5.

ASK YOURSELF: Have you found that people use different language when commenting on a female employee's behaviour versus the same conduct in her male counterpart?

Can you give examples of such instances?

ASK YOURSELF: Do you think you have a bias towards someone of a different gender or even a different race? How are you going to overcome this bias?

CHAPTER 6

OVERCOMING THE FEAR OF ASKING

Earlier on, we looked at how executives need to be encouraged to say YES to accept a new job or promotion. I would now like to dwell a bit on how I have become so aware of the various forms of communication in the corporate environment.

As I have explained, I am blessed with being trilingual and, with being fluent in three languages, I have also adopted three different cultures, cuisines and communication styles. Add a certain amount of international travel to this cocktail and I have been enriched with tolerance for other people's habits and ways. But I digress; the ability to speak three languages has been the key to my moving from academia to corporate. My successive jobs in finance, publishing and telecoms have all relied on this linguistic feature.

Alongside the mastery of different languages has come the awareness that you often have to ASK for what you want.

'You're either remarkable or invisible. Make a choice.' – Seth Godin

Fate would have it that, after the successful acquisition of the video conferencing business, I found myself alone in the lift with Kevin Maxwell, one of Maxwell's sons. It was understood (i.e. nothing in writing) that I would oversee the activities of the new company on behalf of what I call 'The Maxwell Empire'. However, I felt I needed a title to reflect my responsibilities and had made that known to Peter and others, but nothing transpired.

I put my case to Kevin, who responded, 'Do you think my father is the sort of person who is bothered about titles?'

My response was, 'No, but I believe it will be useful both within the company structure and outside when dealing with potential clients of this very new service.' The next day, I was appointed as CEO of Maxwell Satellite Communications. RE-SULT!

Talking about seizing the moment and taking control, this also applied to my early problem of not having a desk – let alone an office. Whilst all the above was happening, I discovered that part of a floor/office space had been vacated. I quickly jumped on the opportunity, obtained some recycled furniture from other parts of the corporation but also took to stealing... It was customary for unwanted furniture to be placed next to the lifts. And so, I often took advantage of this and would return with a new chair for my office and a new desk for one of my colleagues.

'So, all good,' you might say. However, a new opportunity presented itself alongside a serious obstacle to its achievement. Picture this: in 1988, the then DTI (which is now the Department of Business Energy and Industrial Enterprise) decided to deregulate the telecoms/satellite communication industry, which, so far, had been in the hands of British Telecom, Mercury, and Hull. This governmental body proposed to release six licences to six companies in satellite communications. Over twenty-three companies applied, including mammoths like Murdoch's BskyB, Reuters, the BBC itself, Thorn EMI and so on.

Notwithstanding this, my colleagues at Maxwell Satellite said that we should go for it! However, there was one major stumbling block: our backer, Robert Maxwell, had been found by the same governmental body to be unfit to run a public company.

Despite this, we decided to go ahead. In the context of an application like this, you have to:

a. Submit a detailed, considered written submission – and if that is acceptable, you are then invited to
b. make a verbal presentation to the government representatives and answer their questions.

Ultimately, we were shortlisted to meet with the committee. By 'we', I mean the managing director, the technical director and myself. Through my previous contacts at Institutional Investor, I was able to reach out to Alan Watson (now Lord Watson of Richmond) who, at that time, ran a company helping business executives with media presentations. Under his aegis, we rehearsed our presentation and were filmed – which helped to curtail our technical director's wordy enthusiasm!

Time rolled by and then, finally, on the 26th of October (my birthday), it was announced that we had been granted one of these very sought-after licences! Twenty-three companies (including the BBC, Thorn EMI and BSB) had applied for a licence and Maxwell Satellite, a teeny entity compared to these corporate giants, was one of the lucky six licence holders.

Maxwell called me at home that evening (he only called me three times during my entire tenure). He congratulated me on the successful submission and said, in his baritone voice, 'I was advised by David (i.e. Lord Young, who headed up the DTI at the time) that you had succeeded in getting one of the licences, notwithstanding the other applications. I told him I was not surprised; you are prettier and tougher than them.' A double-edged compliment, you might say in this day and age – but you have to understand, we were in the late eighties and it was a fantastic opportunity for a woman to be put in charge.

Ironically, the awarding of the licence was not the end of the story... it turned out that, whilst the DTI had indeed opened up the satellite operations market to six new operators (which included the giant British Aerospace), the licence itself still favoured BT and needed amending. Realising that once one licence was amended, all the other five successful companies would enjoy the same benefits, I volunteered to take the matter forward to the two relevant departments in the European Parliament: Telecoms and Competition.

And so, I did and won. You could say that this is an example of a first ASK having to be followed by a second, and then a third.[62] By that, I mean: we obtained the licence and, when you thought that was the end of the process, we discovered that the licence itself had been amended and that this would involve going to the relevant European departments.

As an executive coach, I now coach my clients to ASK for what they want. Not long ago, I was paired by the Allbright (a female networking club) with Benita, a delightful Spanish lady. This conscientious and rising executive found herself in a good position within a FinTech but was taking on more and more of her boss's responsibilities. Although he was CFO of the company, he was turning his attention to the integration of a new acquisition – from an HR point of view. This left Benita carrying on with her previous tasks and those of the existing CFO. So much so, that any questions relating to the finances of the company would be directly sent to her. She was not uncomfortable with that, but at the same time, she felt that her additional responsibilities were not being recognised. She was also concerned about having her boss fired in the event of a promotion for her. At this point, I took off my coaching cap and put on my mentoring hat and related to her the above story about Kevin and me, and the importance of a title (in and out of a corporate structure).

She took some time to reflect on this and slowly became more confident about putting herself forward. Over some weeks,

---

62   In this respect, I would like to make a personal comment; in 1989, The European Parliament still played a very useful role and I found the relevant departments very open to listening and taking action.

we rehearsed her 'pitch' and also WHO she would pitch – not only the board itself (where she was known) but also other colleagues and, in particular, any female counterparts within the expanding organisation. In other words, she had to learn from male colleagues and adopt their behaviour.

Within a month, Benita was promoted to the role of CFO and her former boss (who had been with the company since its inception) was kept on as a consultant.

So, you will see how I am not only interested in WHAT is said, but also HOW it is said. Saying 'no' is probably the most challenging form of communication, as we will see in the next chapter.

ASK YOURSELF:

Is there something you presently want in your workplace but dare not ask?

Write down a strategy on how – and when – you are going to make that request.

CHAPTER 7

LEARN TO SAY *NO*, ASK FOR HELP, AND SAY *THANK YOU*

In the same way as we need to learn to accept and tackle new tasks, the reverse is equally true. We sometimes need to turn down tasks but how do you say, 'No' to your boss or colleagues?

Very often, a straight negative just doesn't work. I should know! There was a point in my 'Maxwell' years when he saw me as a useful 'tool'. I had managed to obtain this DTI Licence, only years after he had been judged by this same government body as being unfit to run a public company. Mercifully, a friendly colleague tipped me off that he wanted me to join what I called 'the inner sanctum' – his set of personal offices on the fourth floor of the main building. I knew that if I did this, I would be selling my soul and any claim to an identity, so I ducked and dived – and to my relief, the matter of my office transfer was dropped (due to Maxwell's short attention span). Besides, you never say, 'No' to a bully – you find another way around the issue.

As Lois P. Frankel puts it, 'Practice saying, unapologetically, "You know, I'd love to help you out with this, but I'm just swamped." Then stop talking... It's their problem, not yours.'[63] Remember, only *you* can protect your time and prioritise your needs.

In my eleven-plus years as a leadership coach and mentor, I have encountered similar cases where my clients have to disentangle themselves from an undesired situation. Federica, an Italian lawyer, is a good case study. Federica's first mistake was to say 'yes' to her boss when asked to submit her personal mobile number 'in the event of needing you while you're on holiday in the family home in Italy'.

This holiday was a much-needed break for Federica, who was working in a department that should have consisted of four people plus the boss but had been reduced to herself, a colleague and her superior (who did not/could not undertake the more detailed workload). As it was, that colleague left and no attempt appeared to be made to replace her. So, where there should have been four, there were only two.

During her holiday, Federica received countless emails and voice messages from her superior that made her quite visibly distraught. Already a slender woman, she was reduced to a skeleton who had, clearly, not been exposed to the beautiful Ligurian sun. The irony of this is that the boss was also a woman. On hearing the various conversations/exchanges with this boss, I suggested that this female executive was herself a

---

63   Lois P Frankel, PhD, *Nice Girls Do Not Get The Corner Office* (Business Plus, 2014), p. 43.

nervous wreck. She constantly contradicted herself and took the resignation of the staff member personally – referring to her departure as 'treason' and saying she had also had enough and wanted to jump ship and take Federica with her (who was the traitor here?). The next minute, she said that wanted to stay and give Federica a raise...

What could Federica do? Sure, she could change jobs, but that would take a long time, even in those more liquid market conditions. The female boss's own boss sat in Ireland and Federica did not have easy access to him. A direct complaint to HR could easily backfire and provoke the boss's wrath.

I raised the possibility of legal action, but Federica, herself a lawyer, did not wish to go down that route.

Anxious that the conflict between my client and her boss should not appear as a 'catfight' between two female executives, I encouraged Federica to put together a file with all the emails and conversations and, thereby, substantiate her observation regarding her boss's unreasonable behaviour.

In the course of our sessions, I gradually introduced the idea and the method by which Federica would learn to say, 'No' to her exacting boss.

In her instructions to coaches dealing with imposter syndrome sufferers, Tara Halliday invites coaches to encourage the client to 'tell their boss the truth about having too much on their plate ... It is far better to tell the truth and work to make sure the project has every chance of success.'[64]

Failure to decline an assignment can have draining effects; the physical impact of Federica's 'people pleasing' was written all over her increasingly emaciated face.

Another component to saying 'No' is a strong sense of self. As the executive Katie Keith put it to me recently, 'As time goes by and your self-confidence builds, you also realise that you can CHOOSE your employers/clients.'

If, like me, you are aware of your manners and do not wish to come across as rude or disrespectful, check out Grace Hill's book on assertiveness.[65] Being assertive does not mean being aggressive. You can be assertive and remain respectful which, in turn, inspires respect![66]

Hill recommends visualisation to make assertion a part of your life. I would add rehearsing, as exemplified later in this chapter with the case study of Isabella, a hot-headed Italian accountant. Hill also encourages the use of the first person, 'I'

---

64   Tara Halliday, *Unmasking* (p. 185).

65   Grace Hill, *Assertive Communication Skills* (2021). In this book, you
         will come across a 21-day program in Assertiveness Training
         (p. 162 *passim*).

66   Hill, *Assertive Comms*, p. 149.

statements. These show others that you take responsibility for your feelings[67] and do not blame them.

We need to overcome our innate desire to help others and 'make sure that self-care has a higher priority than *giving care*.'[68] We also need to overcome our low self-esteem, desire to be liked and a conflict-averse attitude.

Patrick King offers another insightful strategy, what I would call a compromise. Rather than express a straight 'No', offer a halfway solution, such as: 'I cannot do a full day, but I could offer you two hours.'[69] Alternatively, you may use a deferring technique, requesting more time to decide.

As an illustration of this, a girlfriend of mine, Ines Coupat[70], who transitioned from executive to virtual PA, recognised that she could become more discerning about her clients. After learning to say no, she is now able to focus on the more important projects and channel her talents in their direction. Remember, 'The long-term consequences of putting up with things will far outweigh the short-term discomfort of confrontation.'[71]

Saying 'No' is not a sign of aggression if delivered the right way; it signals your assertiveness. Remember that when you are

---

67   Hill compares in particular the difference of a statement such as 'you make me feel weak when...' to 'I feel weak when...' (p. 37)
68   Zahariades, p. 40.
69   Patrick King, as above, p. 108.
70   Interview of 12/11/2021
71   A Middleton, *Mental Fitness* (p. 290-291).

considering how to decline the job/assignment in question. 'Assertiveness is planned, thoughtful, and considerate.'[72]

Put differently, 'Assertiveness improves interactions with colleagues, family, friends and strangers in all circumstances.'[73] As my fellow coach and friend, Zena Everett, puts it, 'You are saying "no" to the request, not the person.'[74]

Zahariades analyses in detail what stops us from saying, 'No'. One of the fundamental blocks is the belief that it is rude to rebuff a request and that it can lead to disappointment. He teaches the reader to appreciate that [the person's] disappointment is 'neither your fault nor responsibility.'[75] Nor is it about being selfish.

When you have said, 'No,' leave it at that. Adding any other comment will dilute your message and its impact. Remember, in the words of the eminent Warren Buffet, 'The difference between successful people and very successful people is that very successful people say, "No" to almost anything.'[76]

---

72 Damon Zahariades, *The Art of Saying No* (Artofproductivity, 2017), p. 17.
73 Patrick King, *The Art of Everyday Assertiveness* (Amazon, undated), p. 12.
74 Zena Everett, *The Crazy Busy Cure* (Nicholas Brealey Publishing, 2021), p. 65.
75 Zahariades, p. 34.
76 Quoted in *The Art of Saying No*, p. 3.

There is also a side benefit to saying, 'No' and that is that 'people will respect you more'.[77]

Learning to ask for help is as important as learning to say 'No'.

'What is the virtue of saying "No" to help? It's a needless vanity, a failure to recognise change's degree of difficulty.'[78]

'Asking for help is never a sign of failure, but a show of strength and confidence, and knowing your life is worth saving.'[79]

This is an area I have had to work on a lot. The issue stems from my upbringing and the belief, promoted by my French parents living in exile in London, that the three of us constituted a self-sufficient island that needed no assistance from the outside world. They saw asking for help as a sign of weakness that was not something we wished to share.

The eminent professor of management, management consultant and advisor Wayne Baker, comments, '*Not* asking for help is one of the most self-limiting, self-constraining, even self-destructive decisions we can make.' He also quotes a study: 'Failure to ask for help costs *Fortune 500* companies billions of dollars each year.'[80]

---

77   A Middleton, *Mental Fitness* (p. 296).

78   Marshall Goldsmith, *Triggers* (Profile Books, 2016), p. 144.

79   Bündchen, p. 73.

80   Wayne Baker, *All You Have to Do Is Ask* (Currency, 2020), p.5.

Baker shares the eight main reasons that stop us from asking for the things we need.

- We underestimate other people's willingness and ability to help.
- We over-rely on self-reliance.
- We perceive there to be social costs of seeking help.
- Our work culture lacks psychological safety.
- The systems, procedures, or organisational structures get in our way.
- We don't know what to request or how to request it.
- We worry that we haven't earned the privilege of asking for help.
- We fear seeming selfish.[81]

Also, some, like me, are more comfortable *giving* rather than *receiving*. This is ironic because, as a coach and mentor, I encourage my clients to validate their request(s) by thinking of the L'Oréal ad in which Jane Fonda flicks her hair and says, 'Because I'm worth it.'[82] I believe that, once you have that assertion in your head, you then need to determine:

- WHAT to ask
- WHO to talk to
- WHEN to ask

---

81   Baker, p. 16 *passim*.

82   And to any one who thinks I am being sexist, I would remind them that both David Beckham and David Ginola also featured in L'Oréal's campaigns.

To exemplify, Irina had been complaining to me for a while about her workload, her frustration at work and other issues, until, one day, she started talking about her salary and feeling underpaid. At this point, I stopped her and enquired what was REALLY causing her dissatisfaction: the workload? the politics? her bosses? the lack of recognition? or her salary? Of course, you guessed it. At the root of the problem were her earnings. We, therefore, formulated a strategy about who she should make her request to and when. Sometimes, we hide the real issues from ourselves so it pays to step back and use the WHAT? WHO? WHEN? formula.

ASK YOURSELF:

What do you think of the stratagem developed to help Federica?

Let's look at how important it is to say *thank you*. Strangely enough, thanking a person for their offer is also a nice way to decline their help. Phrases like, 'thank you anyway' represent a polite method to turn down somebody's assistance and/or suggestion.

You may recall that, at the beginning of this book, I mentioned how my parents had failed to congratulate me on any of my successes and left me yearning for hugs and some form of recognition. They were also unable to thank me for anything I would do for them – whether preparing a special dish or going on an out-of-the-way errand to satisfy their latest whim. They took pride in their lack of manners – which was all the more ironic, as it had been beaten into me (sometimes literally) to say, 'Thank you.' As I grew older, I would parody their silent ingratitude by parading around the room saying, *'Merci Catherine! Merci Catherine!'*, sometimes followed by a curtsey.

As I share in my coaching, there are always things to be learnt from occasionally hurtful, negative experiences. As a result of their behaviour towards me, I now make a point of writing my thanks to anyone who goes out of their way to help. I also noticed the positive impact that Christopher Harding's missives – sent in his guise of Chairman of British Nuclear Fuels – had on the company's employees. Little did I know that I would eventually end up being a recipient, myself!

Last year, the NHS referred me to a physiotherapist who assisted me with two successive fractured tibias. He was delighted that I took the trouble to write to his head office to compliment his perceptive treatment. Little did I know that, some six months later, he would again be appointed to me, following another fracture. Thanking someone is more relational and less transactional; it plants seeds and can lead to the most surprising outcomes.

This is what happened when my father and I were invited to a fundraising barbeque in the garden of the care home where Anne-Marie was staying.[83] During this very pleasant gathering, my father had a heart attack. The janitor noticed and immediately went into action; it is my firm belief that his intervention saved my father's life. I later wrote a letter to the home's manager commending the alacrity of all the staff, especially this young man, who was medically trained. The manager in turn asked me if I would allow her to forward my missive to her superiors at the NHS – which I gladly accepted. The little piece of paper I had written in gratitude ultimately resulted in the home winning a special award at a black-tie dinner at the prestigious Emirates Stadium. As a thank you for my note, they in turn invited me to join them at their table. It gave me such pleasure to see these people, decked out in all their finery, enjoying the occasion. This array of staff – at all levels of employment – who work so hard and selflessly, receiving a recognition they will never forget. And all because of a simple letter.

More recently, I attended another black-tie dinner (no, that does not happen to me every day!) for eighty people. I was amazed by the quality of the food and the excellent service and commented to this effect to the main organiser. She was delighted to hear my comments and asked me to send her an email, which she would send on to her boss, who was ill

---

83   I have written an extended version of this story – with supporting photos – in https://drcatherinecoaching.com/how-a-little-thank-you-can-make-a-world-of-difference/

with COVID at the time. I was more than happy to do so and mentioned the excellent food and its excellent, swan-like delivery.

We know how to write to complain but forget to pen a thank-you for a job well done. Let's do it more!

ASK YOURSELF:

When was the last time you wrote a thank you note?

Who would benefit from a vote of thanks in your workplace?

LEARN TO APOLOGISE

This is particularly powerfully when dealing with associates and fellow employees. It demonstrates one of the three HUMs promoted by Professor Roger Steare: HUMility.

While it's good to learn how to say, 'No' when necessary, ask for help on occasion, and say, 'Thank you' often, it's important to consider the content of your message.

Marshall Goldsmith relates the story of Sachi,[84] who made the enormous leap from living in a a small village in India, to being a rising tech executive with a Stanford MBA. When reunited with some of her old village friends, she was asked what she had done the preceding week and responded with the truth, which included a recent trip to Paris and meetings with high-flyers. This alienated her old chums who could not relate. She realised that she'd been insensitive. After that, she learned to play down her situation when required.

If you are over-worked and feel you need an assistant or additional member of staff, SAY SO. But, in the same measure, ensure your message is clear; be as precise as you can. If you want a raise, say so.

This may require some soul-searching. One of my clients was ranting and raving about his discontent in his job: how he was asked by his superiors to train new staff; how he was not being given the tasks he wished to concentrate on and felt

---

84   Marshall Goldsmith, *Triggers* (Profile Books, 2016), pp 81-83.

stuck in his position. It was only during our fourth session that he brought up the subject of his salary – he also wanted a raise. At this point, I interrupted him (something I rarely do in coaching sessions) and pointed out that he had not brought up that matter previously. Was that what he wanted most of all and would a better salary make his entire job more bearable? If so, he should deliver *that* message and help his bosses understand the reason for his dissatisfaction.

It's important to consider the tone as well as the content of your message. Women need to be particularly vigilant in this respect. The same words uttered by a female executive are received differently when delivered by her male counterpart.

Whilst recently practising with a client, Isabella, on the point she wished to convey to her superior (the partner in an accountancy firm), we looked at not only the message itself but also its delivery. Isabella quickly recognised that her Latin roots meant she sometimes tended to get a little hot under the collar. This would result in her emotions (mainly anger) taking over and diluting the message. So, having agreed *what* she wished to communicate (her dissatisfaction with the partners' behaviour), we agreed on *how* she would express it. By identifying her emotions and clarifying her thoughts, she adopted a new behaviour that enabled her to put her message across clearly and also keep herself in check in the event of any exchange.

Dr Deborah Tannen, in her excellent book, *Talking from 9 to 5*, refers to the language a female technical director for a news/

talk show, Carol, used when dealing with a nervous male replacement in the control tower. Rather than tell or show the technician what to do, she presented all the features as quirks of the company. Thus, rather than saying, 'Don't mix up tapes; make sure you get them in the right order,' she said, 'The only thing that people usually have trouble with is that they end up playing the promos and cassette tags and stuff in the wrong order.' What Carol did was reframe the issue to avoid being condescending with the replacement technician. She got him to relax and absorb the information so that he could perform on the night.[85] Carol chose HOW she was going to deliver the message to him.

ASK YOURSELF:

Have you found yourself in a situation where the answer is not a straight A or B?

What has this Chapter taught you?

---

85   Deborah Tannen, PhD, *Talking 9 To 5* (William Morrow and Company, 1994), p. 138.

CHAPTER 8

NON-VERBAL COMMUNICATIONS: LEARNING TO WATCH AND LISTEN

In the words of my friend, Melissa Lund, stylist and image consultant, 'Clothes have a language. Think carefully about what you want to say before you get dressed.'

I felt it important to underline this in the context of what we express without words.

Your body language also plays a part here:

- Stand up straight
- Keep your hands where they can be seen
- Look straight at the person who is talking
- Don't let your eyes dart all over the room
- Keep your facial expression gentle and offer an honest smile[86]
- Do not lean in, which would appear confrontational
- Listen

Let's focus on the last point. We are sometimes so intent on putting a message across that we fail to hear what the other

---

86   Hill, *Assertive Communications Skills*, p. 69.

person is saying. The failure to listen leads to what I label as 'talking AT'.

Is it not ironic that, when talking about communication, we talk about WAYS to speak, but fail to recognise how important it is to listen?

'Effective communication is not only about talking and sharing; it is also about active listening.'[87] By paying attention to what is being said, you can pick up the person's emotions and moods. It can also help in disagreements.

The concept of active listening was developed by psychologists Carl Rogers and Richard Farson in a 1957 paper, where the actions required are:

- ► listening to the full meaning of a message
- ► responding to emotions
- ► noticing non-verbal communications[88]

James W. Williams lists no less than TWENTY-NINE forms of listening – ranging from Active Listening, Biased Listening, to Whole Person Listening! [89]

---

87 James Turnbull, *The Essential Guide to Assertiveness* (libritopublising, 2021), p. 7.

88 Rogers, Carl R., and Richard Evans Farson, *Active Listening* (Mansfield Centre: Martino Publishing, 1957).

89 James W. Williams, *Listening Skills Training* (Amazon, 2021).

Fundamentally, active listening can only happen if we suspend all judgement and pre-conceptions towards that person, or the subject they are addressing. Additionally, as with bullies, step away from the situation when it becomes confrontational and be aware of your own emotions.

Are there people who rub you up the wrong way? What can you do differently with them? Or should you avoid them at all costs? Take a good honest look at the situation and at how it has arisen.

► Are you able to talk this through with them? Have you tried (now be honest here!)?

It's important use the first person here as in, 'When you do xyz, I feel hurt.'

► What would life look like without them in your world?

► Can someone mediate between the two of you? Harry Truman explains peace in the following terms: 'When we understand the other fellow's viewpoint and he understands ours, then we can sit down and work out our differences.'

► How would ostracising that person affect those around you?

There are times, such as in difficult conversations, when it is better to keep quiet for a while and reflect on what is being said rather than saying something yourself. There is nothing to be gained by starting a verbal slinging match.

I remember one specific instance which illustrates the point. My parents owned a basement flat which they let out to tenants. Unfortunately, the last rental did not last long as the occupants were musicians and the rising dampness made it impossible for them to keep their instruments in the apartment for fear of damage. I recall taking René (my father) to the flat to show him the visible damp patches. Rather than address the issue, he turned on me, shouting that I had no need to shout...

Indeed, I had certainly raised my voice as he was deaf and did not always wear his hearing aids (if at all) at the right volume. I did not respond. I understood that his loud retort was caused, not by the timbre of my voice, but by the fact that he was embarrassed to witness the degradation of the flat – which was very much due to his reluctance to maintain the property in any shape or form. The incident was witnessed by a friend, who later commented on my silence (and apparent placidity). I explained the sub-text to René's outburst. My friend marvelled at my ability to stay calm in such a situation; I explained that it came from years of actively listening and learning to decipher the real message behind the words. This is also, by the way, a technique that comes in very useful when dealing with bullies. No wonder there is the saying, 'Do not shoot the messenger...'

When you are upset by someone's regular lateness, rather than blurting out, 'You are late again!' talk about how their unpunctuality makes you feel. Let them know:

- ► The situation
- ► How you feel about it

- ► What you need or desire from them
- ► Its consequences[90]

I recently discussed the subject of tacit communications in my very first Zoom call with the charming Kriss Akabusi MBE, Olympian Champion and now coach. In his characteristic incisive manner, he then turned the question round and asked me what the background behind me 'said' about my character and tastes.

A question I had never been asked!

So, I turned round and looked at this particular bookcase, which was adorned with cookery and travel books, a silver tray, a couple of bottles, some photos and crystalware. As I remained silent, he probed further, focused on the silver tray and enquired about its purpose. I explained it was one of two (its twin is displayed on the shelf opposite) and that these trays would come out in the hands of a butler – hired for the evening – when either my parents or myself entertained. Otherwise, they proudly stood on a stand.

From this, he concluded that I was quite a 'social animal' – which sums me up perfectly! The background behind me 'betrayed' more about me than I could ever convey in words; it, alone, told a story. It is something worth considering as we all make increasing use of Zoom/Teams/FaceTime!

---

90   Turnbull, p. 97.

The subject of bookcases leads me to mention Ladey Adey's initiative to include a photo of members' bookcases – which she calls 'shelfies'. Mine (different to the one observed by Kriss) points to my early academic life and my present coaching interests. The top shelves are occupied by Ancient Greek/ French and Latin/French dictionaries – as well as full editions published by La Pléiade. The books in the La Pléiade collection are all a leather bound, stamped in gold on the spine, enclosing a text block on bible paper – they pay homage to France's top French writers and poets, as well as my French education. The lower shelves bear testimony to my present interest in self-development and coaching with writings from the likes of Daniel Goleman, Valerie Young and others.

Photos also provide insights into a person's interests; some three months ago, a friend called me requesting my urgent help with his suicidal son aged 14. Given the emergency, I suggested they come straight to my flat. I do not usually see clients at home but the occasion required a quick response. So, I met Finley in my sitting room; over the two hours together, there were tears and silences with him casting his gaze around the room. His attention was particularly drawn to a photo of myself (in a red dress) surrounded by five Chelsea Pensioners in their usual red regalia. Finley enquired what my attachment was to the military; I explained I was a guest of Barclays Bank that day – as were the Pensioners and we all sat in the same section of the 02 arena. I added that I was part of Barclays AFTER programme helping former service people navigate their way into civilian life. From there, he started to tell me about his interest in joining the Army.

That photo opened up a whole new side to his personality and, as it happens, got Finley thinking about his aspirations for the future – a mile away from his suicidal thoughts....[91]

As the saying goes, a picture is worth a thousand words!

ASK YOURSELF:

Thinking back on an incident where your emotions took over and you failed to communicate your message clearly, what would you do differently now?

ASK YOURSELF:

Take a look at your present backdrop on Zoom/ Team calls. What should you change?

---

91   As a result of this urgent consultation, Finley agreed to see a psychiatrist and undergo specialist care.

CHAPTER 9

WHEN NETWORKING IS CONNECTING

In Chapter 3, I related how my previous connection with Peter Laister gave me a lifeline in the Maxwell empire. If you ever needed proof of the importance of networking, you have it there in one single incident!

Years ago, during an annual conference for Institutional Investor in Puerto Rico, I was asked to give a presentation on networking, which I duly delivered with no further thought. It was only years later that I realised that I had been invited to speak on that subject because I was quite good at it (I can be quite slow at times!) This has given rise to my thinking about the key elements of networking, which I will share with you now.

I will start by saying that I do not like the word 'networking'. As a linguist and businesswoman, it has, for me, all sorts of negative connotations. I prefer the term 'connecting' and that is how I approach things.

In his excellent book on the subject, Charlie Lawson[92] poses the question of whether networking fits better with an introvert or an extrovert.

---

92 *The Unnatural Networker*, Charlie Lawson, Panoma Press, 2014.

At first glance, you might think the extrovert – surely – but then, on reflection, you might reconsider that conclusion. That is because networking is not about how many people you meet, but about listening. It is not about 'working' a (chat) room and collecting business cards or LinkedIn contacts. It is about creating links forged over time, and who better to listen than an introvert?

The gift which introverts hold is best expressed in the title of Susan Cain's book, *Quiet: The Power of Introverts in a World That Can't Stop Talking*!

Growing up, I was very shy. My domineering mother ensured that I was only to speak when spoken to. So, I resorted to listening and watching people. I developed a genuine curiosity about what makes people tick, their postures and intonations.

This has served me well, for it is this genuine interest in people that has enabled me to network – or rather, connect – my way around the world (and has also allowed me to be an effective coach and mentor). In their book *How Women Rise*, Sally Helgesen and Marshall Goldsmith[93] underline the importance of connections in the business world: 'Connections serve as a kind of currency you can use to get resources moving and ensure your contributions are noticed.'

Debbie Wosskow and Anna Jones founded The Allbright on the basis that women need more help in networking than men. Raimonda Jankunaite in turn set up the Women In Business Club.

---

93   As before, p. 93.

However, whether you're male or female, here are my key rules regarding networking.

Rule No. One:

Remember, no one goes to a networking event to buy your product. Save yourself some effort and time-wasting by listening and taking a keen interest in what is being said. In other words, start building a relationship and mutual trust. As Ivan Meisner puts it, 'Ask questions'.[94]

Handy tip:

As soon as you can, make notes of what has been said – Sophia's hobbies, children, favourite holiday destination. I enter these notes in my electronic contact book under Notes. I use these notes in all sorts of ways. For instance, in my follow-up note to our first meeting, I refer to our conversation, whilst still being mindful of GDPR.[95]

Rule No. Two:

Ensure that you introduce yourself with an explanation of what you do – not a title/description. For instance, I could say, 'Hi,

---

94   Ivan Misner, PhD, *Networking Like A Pro, Entrepreneur Press, 2009,* p. 21.

95   GDPR stands for General Data Protection Regulation, adopted by both the European Union and the UK to constrain companies' ability to mine digital records without the consumers' consent.

I am a graphic designer', or I could say, 'Hi, I help people and companies create their own memorable brand.'

Rule No. Three:

Recognise that non-business-related events can also create valuable contacts. Consider charities or hobbies that you follow. I go even further – a habit I acquired from my ex, Christopher. If I am going to a social gathering, such as a dinner, I ask the host who the other guests are – not because I want to 'hit' on them, but so that I can have an idea of what might interest them and how I might best engage with them.

NB: I have to say that this approach does not go down well with everyone. Not long ago, I was invited to join a birthday party dinner by a person I had only met twice and could not even remember. I made the type of enquiry I described above only to be told, 'It is only a meeting of friends.' Well, since I did not qualify as a friend, I did not think I was unjustified in asking the question... The moral of this anecdote is that my tactics might not always work with people outside of the working environment.

Rule No. Four:

Be sure to drop your new contact an email within 24 hours of your first meeting and suggest a second one where you might exchange business ideas. Have you thought of someone they would like to meet? Mention this as well. Your follow-up is even more crucial than the initial contact.

Phrases like, 'I would like to hear more about your business' and, 'I would like to see how I can help you' are good openers. Or, 'I wondered if I could have your advice on...' Remember, people love being asked for their opinion.

Also, be sure to 'connect' with them on LinkedIn with a note referring back to your original meeting.

Rule No. Five:

Once you are sure Sophia is someone you would trust, feel free to open up your address book to her.

Think laterally; connections can come from all sorts of aspects of your life! Only recently, I met a delightful man, Peter, on a dating website. In the course of our conversation, it transpired that he was an aeronautical engineer with a keen interest in cars and racing. It happens that one of my business contacts was setting up a new business with several bespoke cars. I put the two together and they are presently negotiating a working arrangement between them.

So, you see, it does not matter where you are, or where you meet people. Even a blind date can be a networking opportunity.

Rule No. Six:

Keep in touch! Imagine the press has written a favourable article about a contact's company; send them an email about the coverage.

I did this recently with one of my clients who is being considered for an important PR job at Santander bank. I alerted her to the fact that a very glowing article had appeared on the CEO, Ana Botin, and suggested that she drop her contact at the bank a little note. In this way, she managed to:

- ► show her ongoing interest in the bank
- ► remind her contact of her existence and keep herself present in their mind
- ► demonstrate her ability to digest press coverage

LinkedIn:

LinkedIn provides an excellent way of keeping in touch, as well as being a first-class tool to prepare for an eventual introduction.

A. Keeping in touch on LinkedIn:

What can be easier than to like an article posted by your new contact? If you can, add a comment as well!

B. Using LinkedIn to prepare an introduction:

Now, having covered some generalities about the meeting itself, let us go back in time and consider the preparation.

Before the Event:

Sometimes, event organisers will publish/release the list of speakers as well as attendees prior to a meeting. I go through these names and send them a message on LinkedIn asking them to connect, stating, 'Looking forward to meeting at the XXXX conference.' You will be surprised how easy that makes it for you to go up to them at the conference and make physical contact: 'Hi, I am Catherine. I sent you an email via LinkedIn...' and the conversation will flow from there. Who needs an ice-breaker?

I did this recently with the super-busy Vanessa Vallely of We Are The City. She was speaking at a Women of Influence conference (part of Cancer Research UK, where we are both mentors). After a year of trying to meet her through mutual contacts and a long exchange of emails, I sent her an email through LinkedIn, explaining that I was looking forward to finally meeting her and discussing the series of articles I was proposing for her organisation.

Thus, when I met Vanessa, she immediately knew what my interest was and put me in touch with her editorial team. How good is that?

If you have the list of delegates before the meeting, earmark those people you would like to meet, and ask one of the organisers if they can introduce you. BUT REMEMBER RULE 1 – do not attempt to sell them anything if you have never met or dealt with them before. In this respect, my approach to Vanessa V. is not a contradiction as I had already been in an e-exchange with her for a good 12 months. Furthermore, she is a very busy woman...

Now, before you enter the room:

What to wear?

1. Clothes:

Remember, clothes are as much a language as the words you use. Sad as it is, people WILL judge you if your dress is inappropriate to their norms; a T-shirt and jeans will not go down well with a group of barristers, any more than an evening gown/black tie would be acceptable to a bunch of hippies. Remember, you have between five and thirty seconds for people to judge you.

That said, do not be afraid to stand out from the crowd. Today being a sunny day in early May, I am wearing a sharp yellow trouser suit over a black top with black accessories. I also often wear a distinctive 'colour' to an event – a white dress – it makes it easier for the organiser to find me in the room and point me out to the person I have asked to meet.

For you, gentlemen, it might be a pink shirt or a striking tie. And remember, people might gravitate to you because of the colour of your shirt.

2. Badge:

Some organisers are very casual about their delegates' badges – providing mere see-through badge holders in which to include your business card or stick-on labels.

I hate both, so I have commissioned my loyal printer, Les Bexfield at Westlandprint, to make up a magnetic badge for me which I keep in my handbag and use as and when I feel appropriate.

3. A pen or mobile:

You will need to make notes sooner or later about the information you have garnered: a delegate/speaker, or a reminder concerning his hobbies/habits. At this point, your favourite form of note-taking comes into play: a pencil/pen or straight into your mobile.

4. Business card:

Speaking last year at Cancer Research's Women of Influence, I was shocked to learn how few of these eminent lady scientists had a business card... All I can say – and did say – is, if your job will not pay for it, go to an online printer like Moo and have some cards printed with your basic details. There is also an electronic card made by V1CE, which transmits all your details with one tap, including your socials.

5. Handbag:

For the ladies, do not carry a clutch bag. Imagine juggling your clutch bag, your cup of coffee/glass of champagne, a canapé and shaking hands – all at the same time!

We might be multi-taskers, but no. Wear a bag preferably with a shoulder strap from which you can easily extricate your business card/mobile phone.

Right! So we are now fully clothed, armed with pen/mobile/ visiting cards; only one further thing is left to carry in with you:

6. Smile:[96]

Be sure to enter the room with a smile. I cannot over-accentuate the importance of this feature! Do you want to meet a grumpy person? No!? Show your warmth with a smile! As Ivan Meisner puts it, 'Studies have shown that if you smile when you talk, you seem more open and forthright.'[97]

Are you nervous? Smile! Forget the wrinkles! SMILE... Then, sometimes after the smile, comes the introduction.

7. How to break into a group:

Look around the room and decide for yourself which group you would like to target. Aim for one that looks open – as opposed to a closed, intense, one-to-one. I then just simply ask, 'May I join you?'

8. Introduction:

At this point, the introduction might well come from you holding out your hand – or someone extending theirs. Whatever the case, be sure to exchange a firm handshake; I am not talking about a crippling greeting, but a firm handshake, with eye contact. Announce your name clearly.[98] As Lois P.

96 See Chapter 11, *'Is Humour a Form of Control?'*.

97 Ivan Misner, p. 93.

98 Lois P. Frankel, p. 119.

Frankel puts it, 'Although you do not want to develop a bone-crushing grasp, you do want to be certain that your handshake conveys the message, "I'm someone to be taken seriously."'[7] And be sure to make eye contact. 'If the eyes are the window to the soul, then you must use them to allow others to see your sincerity, self-confidence, and knowledge, and to see the other person's.'[99]

9. What do you do?

At this point, someone is likely to ask you, 'What do you do?' Unless you are a carpenter or a plumber (no disrespect to this industry), your interlocutor may not understand the sort of response I used to give, such as, 'I am a leadership consultant'. If I was lucky, I'd get a few well-meaning nods to this.

I have now learnt to respond by saying WHAT I DO – as opposed to WHAT I AM – i.e., 'I help leaders become better leaders...it can be very lonely at the top and leaders need an impartial person with whom they can discuss their issues.'

10. How to make an exit?:

We have all experienced this. You want to get out of the conversation you are in.

I recall Viscount Linley (now Lord Linley), the Queen's nephew, wanting to get rid of me at a function and he just pointed out, 'Oh, I can see there is a person over there who wants to talk to you.' A clever ploy, but not one that I could carry off, I admit.

---

99   Lois P. Frankel, p. 291.

I sometimes invite the person I am talking with to join me in another group: 'Shall we go and network over there? Would you like to come with me?'

Or I will be more direct: 'It has been nice talking to you – and here is my card.'

11. Online networking – LinkedIn/Facebook/Twitter/ Instagram/Zoom:

Be sure to reach out to your new connections on LinkedIn and maybe even reach out on LinkedIn through a special application to all those present in the room.

You also need to consider your profile:

- Include a photo
- Explain what you DO rather than your job title
- Post content regularly. Aim for once a week
- Comment/like other's content

12. Once you are in contact:

Make a note of their secretary's name and what HER interests are. I lodge this information in the notes section of my contact book, alongside the boss' hobbies, etc.[100] Remember, the secretary is the person who will put you through to the boss; (s)he alone decides whether you are worthy of the boss' time, so establish a rapport there too.

---

100 See above …

In their analysis of 'power', Sally Helgesen and Marshall Goldsmith[101] comment, 'Connections serve as a kind of currency you can use to get resources moving and assure your contributions get noticed.' When I was preparing for my live job interview with Maxwell, I called on different contacts of mine to find out what he was like and what I could expect from the (then) great man. Fate would have it that at least one of these people – the CEO of an international advertising agency – reported this back to him and he specifically reported in the programme that my research had greatly impressed him.

Others refer to networking as social capital,[102] quoting the fictional character of Don Draper in *Mad Men* saying, 'Contacts mean contracts'.

Finally, and not least, remember to thank anyone who gives a referral that turns into business.

13. Networking and the sexes:

We have to recognise that men presently have the upper hand in networking. In the words of Mary Portas, 'If corporate networking goes on in the pub after work and you're a mother who needs to get home for childcare, or all the supervisors at the factory... are men who play in the same football team, you're starting at second-generation gender bias.'[103] However, this is changing.

---

101 *How Women Rise*, p. 93.
102 Premuzic, p. 109.
103 Portas, p. 21.

That said, we can all learn from one another. 'When women network, they are working as gatherers, planting seeds and acquiring friends, not using transactional friends the way men do, but actual friends... Men need to become more adept at building real relationships... Women, on the other hand, would do well to focus on extracting some transactions from their business relationships. They must keep in mind what the purpose of business networking is.'[104] Female executives also need to build credibility fast, by letting their male counterparts know what they have achieved and how they can help them.

Case Study – Connecting is not an overnight affair:

I met the eminent Dr Colin Brewer in the early eighties at a cocktail party. Since then, our social paths have crossed now and then and I have sent him the odd email about a subject pertinent to his work, or a mutual connection. There was no after-thought to this; only the desire to keep in touch. As it is, I have recently been diagnosed with an illness which is one of his specialisations. I called him and he invited me to his home within a week to discuss this matter.[105] He is now helping me and, in return, I am a volunteer for one of his research projects. You just never know! Ant Middleton uses similar language and elaborates, 'You never know what the opportunity is until it arrives. All you can do is make yourself the best version of

---

104 Ivan Misner, *Business Networking And Sex* (Entrerpreneur Media, 2012), p. 79.
105 See closing chapter ....

yourself that you can so that when the moment arrives, you can seize it.'[106]

The ultimate challenge is reaching out to a person you do not know and with whom you have no mutual connection:

Over the years, I have developed an approach that my husband called 'Catherine's cheeky email'. It is based on the ability to read and apply the recently acquired information in a short, well-targeted email. Just as active listening is important, so too is attentive reading.

I was recently prompted to write to James Timpson, CEO of Timpson, concerning an article he wrote in the business section of *The Sunday Times*. In it, he stated that he sends thirty hand-written letters a week. This very much resonated with me, as one of my top communication tips underlines the importance of saying, 'Thank you'. But, how to reach him? The Timpson website only leads to their retail services; there's nothing at all relating to the board or their PR/communications team.

LinkedIn came to my rescue. There, I found listings for a couple of employees. I wrote to each of them, explaining that I was looking for the CEO's email address, with the reason why. I also sent them a link to the blog I had written a while ago illustrating the power of a thank-you letter. I am delighted to say that they all replied and one of them provided me with the required information. I sent off my email on Friday.

---

106 Ant Middleton, *Zero Negativity* (Harper.Collins, 2011), p. 210 +
     Chapter 10 of *Mental Fitness*

On Sunday evening (no less), I received a reply from James Timpson himself, apologising for the 'late reply'(!) and putting me in touch with one of the company directors – whom I had already contacted via LinkedIn. Thus, my strategy had a successful outcome!

Real networking involves a long-term commitment on your behalf. To use a metaphor used by Business Network International, it is about 'farming', not 'hunting'. For me, networking is not about accumulating addresses; it is about MAKING CONNECTIONS. I often liken 'networking' to an act of seduction. It does not happen overnight, but rose by rose, petal by petal...

ASK YOURSELF:

Who should I include in my network?

How am I going to keep in touch with them?

CHAPTER 10

DRESS FOR SUCCESS

It will not surprise you to hear that your inward confidence can be enhanced by your outward appearance. Making an impact when walking into a room is important – whether we are dating, attending a conference or meeting with the boss.

When we are feeling down, we withdraw into ourselves and physically shrink. Our gaze is downward facing and our shoulders are shrugged. This is when you need to look up, take the first step forward, pull your shoulders back ... and SMILE. Think, 'Presentation Smile!'

Science tells us that it takes seven seconds to make a first impression, so be sure to make the right impact.

Marie Ann Sieghart quotes Dame Sarah Mullaly, the first-ever female Bishop of London. 'If I'm going somewhere that I think will be tough, I pull my shoulders back... And if it is a tough meeting, I'll wear red lipstick.'[107]

---

107 Mary Ann Sieghart, p. 103.

The ethereally beautiful actress Kristen Scott Thomas admitted in an interview with *The Daily Mail*[108] that, as she approaches middle age, she feels invisible. 'Somehow, you just vanish. It's a cliché, but men grow in gravitas as they get older, while women just disappear... I'm not talking about in a private setting, at a dinner party, or anything. But, when you're walking down the street, you get bumped into, people slam doors in your face – they just don't notice you.'

As much as I admire her as an actress, I do not agree with her on this point. It is up to us to present ourselves in the right light and to dare to go forward.

We ladies are lucky in that we have a larger array of clothes and colours to choose from than men do. I have always favoured flamboyant (and you might say, assertive) colours: orange, fuchsia, red, yellow, turquoise – or white! As Mary Portas puts it, 'I leave the house knowing that what I'm wearing is a reflection of me – colourful, confident and slightly flamboyant.'[109] Rita Clifton, of Saatchi & Saatchi fame, makes the same point. Whilst on a trip to Italy, she developed what she called 'jacket it is' when she came across a jacket in a shop that fitted perfectly and was also 'confidence boosting'. She comments how '...it's good to have an interesting feature

---

108 https://www.dailymail.co.uk/tvshowbiz/article-2380539/Kristin-Scott-Thomas-I-invisible-like-middle-aged-women.html.

109 Mary Portas, *Work Like A Woman* (Penguin, 2018), p. 11.

of some kind (colour, shape...) so that you don't fall into the conventional corporate uniform department.'[110]

We also have another tool up our sleeves: shoes! For me, it is high heels, as reported not long ago in *The Daily Mail*.[111] They make me feel good and improve my posture no end! Mary Beard even goes as far as to interpret Teresa May's, '... "shoe thing" and those kitten heels are one of the ways she shows that she is refusing to be packaged into the male template.'[112] She makes a similar comment about Margaret Thatcher's handbags,[113] but, interestingly enough, does not comment on our present Queen's! I ask myself if that is because she does not think HRH Elizabeth II is a woman of power, or whether she prefers not to talk about the present monarch for fear of being dragged to the Tower of London!

Helena Morrissey, top financier, mother of nine and now author of *Style and Substance*, echoes my own feelings about colour and heels and adds to the discussion with the importance of wearing make-up if you are a woman.

Whilst carrying out research around this part of the book, I was struck by how several authors and journalists have commented on how our appearance can be equalled to a form of branding.

---

110 Rita Clifton, *Love Your... Imposter* (Kogan Page, 2020), p. 50.

111 https://www.dailymail.co.uk/femail/article-9917137/Meet-Britains-heeled-women-Meet-shoe-addicts-giving-Imelda-Marcos-run-money.html.

112 Mary Beard, p. 82.

113 Mary Beard, p. 82.

Morrissey uses the word outright:[114] 'My personal brand... has evolved to be deliberately more impactful, even exuberant, to meet my goals.' Theresa May's shoes, Mrs Thatcher's handbags, and Lady Hale's animal brooches can all be viewed as forms of branding. I prefer to use the word 'style'.

As Polonius puts it to Laertes in *Hamlet*, 'The apparel oft proclaims the man.' Your choice of dress and accessories can also send out deliberate messages. I was fascinated to learn that Secretary Madeleine Albright used her brooches to communicate her defiance to her counterparts; for instance, she wore a serpent brooch when addressing a press conference around the then-Iraqi situation – all because Saddam had called her a serpent. Similarly, when it was discovered that the Russians had bugged the State Department, she wore an enormous bug pin for her meeting with the Russian foreign minister. This tacit communication ultimately led to more productive conversation.[115]

I recently attended a CEO dinner and talk where I met a group of charming young executives, who were attracted to me (I later learnt) by the electric blue tuxedo suit that I was wearing. One of them, Christine Kitching of Marquee Brands, commented, 'As women, we have to take extra care in our personal presentation. An outfit is key to making you feel

---

114 Morrissey, Helen quoted in the *DMail's Inspire*, Oct 8th 2021.
115 Aaker, Bagdonas, p. 149.

your best self. More than half of it, in my opinion!'[116] Christine was kind enough to go even further: 'Bold, confident [sic] and inspirational. Three words that came to mind when spotting Dr Catherine at a CEO event I was attending. Catherine's personal presentation in an imperial blue suit screamed "Fierce Female Warrior" to me. Coincidentally, I too had selected a suit in the same colour to wear as a speaker. I picked that ensemble to give off the same vibes that Catherine gave off when entering the room. Empowered, strong, confident and together!'

Regardless of the colour, I always choose clothes I am comfortable in. Whatever the meeting, your mobility and temperature are important.

You also have to consider the dress code. In the eighties, women did NOT wear trousers to meetings. It was so much so that, should I turn up to the office wearing slacks, my colleagues would interject, 'Oh Catherine, I can see you do not have any meetings today.' Remember, what you wear is a form of communication. Things have evolved a lot today with regard to the female dress code; as Mary Beard comments, 'a powerful woman... looks rather like a man'[117] and illustrates the point with a photo of Angela Merkel hugging Hilary Clinton in what she refers to as 'their female politicians' uniform'. Gill Whitty-Collins goes even further by suggesting that Hilary's 'copying' her male counterparts' form of dress showed her

---

116 Christine Kitching, Vice President, International Business
     Development & Partnerships, Marquee Brands.
117 Mary Beard, p. 54-5.

to lack authenticity and probably contributed to her failure in becoming the next US president.[118] Conversely, *Forbes* magazine believes that Merkel's 'frumpy style ... had proved an asset to her career'.[119]

Lois P. Frankel compares the impact of appearance, voice and content. 'Research shows that about fifty-five percent of your credibility comes from how you look. How you sound accounts for an additional thirty-eight percent. Only seven percent of your credibility is based on what you say.'[120]

If you are in doubt as to how 'dress makes the man',[121] dwell for a moment on one of my bug-bears – how a uniform can affect a person's behaviour. Have you ever come across customs (or police) officers who feel that their very uniform gives them the right to challenge your credentials? They become mini-dictators with enhanced self-importance. In these instances, they have no choice as to what they wear; it is a uniform. But, ironically, although they do not have a say in their clothing, they believe their stature is enhanced.

---

118 Gill Whitty-Collins, *Why Men Win At Work* (Luath Press Ltd, p.2021), p. 69.

119 Forbes.com 2016, *Power Dressing: How Women Politicians use Fashion.*

120 Lois P Frankel, p. 263.

121 You might like to know that the comment originates from Mark Twain. The full quote is: 'Clothes make the man. Naked people have little or no influence on society.'

I have already talked about clothes and shoes, but other smaller items also deserve attention such as the pen and stationery you are using. A disposable hotel ballpoint pen and notepad might not convey the best message. Conversely, armed with a good pen and stationery, you are ahead of the game in the confidence stakes. This is a predilection of mine; I call these accessories my 'toys'. They are invariably burgundy coloured, whether branded or not.

ASK YOURSELF:

Do you take your appearance into consideration when you have a meeting/interview?

Are you aware of the impact it makes?

What should you be doing differently?

CHAPTER 11

IS HUMOUR A FORM OF CONTROL?

Throughout my childhood and adulthood, my parents would pick on my laughter: 'Oh Catherine, *ce rire!*' ('Oh Catherine, THAT laugh!'). On the other hand, friends and strangers have told me that my laugh is certainly distinctive, and even infectious.

Faced with this conflicting feedback, my PhD thesis included various analyses of the effect of laughter and humour. In my thesis, I devoted a few pages to laughter – greatly inspired by the writings of Henri Bergson.[122] A lot more has been written on the subject since then; some of which is even in the context of management/leadership. My preferred contribution is by Roger Steare, who describes the three 'ingredients' of leadership as the three Hums:

- ► HUMility
- ► HUManity
- ► HUMour

Humour is a device I have used a lot when addressing bullies, or just dealing with difficult situations. Whitty-Collins quotes

---

122 Bergson, Henri,. *Le Rire.* 7th edition. Paris, Felix Alcan, 1911.

two female executives as saying, 'Making the point with firmness and, sometimes, even some ironic humour can often be more effective than a confrontational approach,' and 'I don't like conflict and my first defence mechanism is humour and sarcasm.'[123]

At the time, I did not realise it was a 'tool' – it only came to me much later on that my play on words, or my 'riposte' was using humour.

'Humor is a vital tool of leadership,' says Dr Gerald D. Bell, the founder and CEO of Bell Leadership Institute. 'People are used to associating laughter with the best medicine, but they are often surprised that "sense of humor" is the phrase most frequently associated with the best in leaders.' Bell's leadership findings show that people appreciate leaders who have fun and work hard to get the job done. 'Those who can combine a strong work ethic and sense of humor may have the leading edge in their organizations,' says Dr Bell.[124] Such is the importance of humour that Hill dedicates a full day to it in his 21-day program that deals with assertive communications.

More recently, Brighton Girls' school introduced laughing classes for its pupils to combat stress and anxiety. I have also read that the NHS is looking at offering similar classes for patients suffering from depression.

---

123 Whitty-Collins, p. 135.
124 https://www.bellleadership.com/humor-gives-leaders-edge/

I rarely use humour in my coaching sessions. That said, there is one instance where I did highlight the comical aspect of a situation: Norman was in his mid-20s and, after working as a second-hand car salesman, he was considering moving into real estate, commenting, 'It could hardly get worse,' to which I retorted, 'Well, I do not know, you could always try selling double-glazing.' This young man looked at me, stunned, and exploded in laughter. Unwittingly, I had exposed a human side to my character – one which transcended age and coach-coachee roles.

Humour is effective in two ways – it benefits us as the originator of the humour and it has a favourable effect on the audience. 'By encouraging humour and banter, barriers are more likely to be broken.'[125]

'When we refuse to take ourselves so seriously… we create more meaningful connections with our colleagues and open our minds to more innovative solutions.'[126] Humour is not international and, when using it, one must be mindful if it is appropriate to that country's culture. That said, I personally favour self-deprecation. In one of my jobs, where I bore the title of 'Managing Director,' I renamed myself 'Damaging Director.' Since then, I have deliberately coined the phrase when referring to a person's boss. It reveals that I am on their

---

125 Dobson, p. 155.

126 Jennifer Aaker and Naomi Bagdonas, *Why Humor is a Secret Weapon in Business and Life And How Anyone Can Harness It, Even You* (Currency, 2020), p. 6.

side, without having to say too much and, thus, creates a bond between us.

In the same vein, my recent coaching sessions have taken me away from traditional coaching to assisting executives with their business strategies. It has made me realise that part of my offering could be that of a business strategist, or BS (as in bulls**tter) – as I like to quip...

I have also used humour in social situations to hide my emotions. Not long ago, I was invited to a lunch in the Westfield shopping centre in West London. I arrived late for a series of reasons, including having to find a mobility scooter to take me to the appropriate (and most distant) section of the mall. Irritated with myself for being an hour late, knowing there were six or more strangers at the table, I 'drove' myself in and quipped whilst 'disembarking' from the scooter, 'I hope they accept off-street parking.' No great joke, you might say, but it served to put me at ease and to convey that I did not take myself too seriously.

Humour is also a powerful leadership strategy and can play an even bigger role for leaders: it shatters barriers and authority. The late Prince Philip's legendary gaffes are a brilliant example of using humour as ice-breakers. They were often a deliberate mechanism on his part to put people at ease. As Aaker and Bagdonas put it, levity creates balance.[127]

---

127 Aaker, Bagdonas, p. 26.

Above all (and this is where I get a bit controversial), I believe humour is a source of control. It enables you to increase:

► Power – a clever repartee can help you regain your presence in the room.
► Bonds – Laughter triggers the release of oxytocin, often referred to as the 'trust hormone'.[128]
► Creativity – Fear paralyses; humour relaxes; by reducing stress, humour makes us feel safer, calmer and releases our creativity.
► Resilience.[129] 'Humour doesn't just help reduce stress, though; it also helps people cope in times of acute distress.'[130] I mentioned how Secretary of State Madeleine Albright's brooches often communicated her defiance to her foreign counterparts.[131] 'Albright consistently used humour to defuse tensions, build personal connections, and lay the groundwork for crucial high-stakes conversations.'[132]

The power of humour is also illustrated in the Aaker-Bagdonas book when they focus on how re-framing our mistakes through a comic lens can impact both our lives[133] and the lives of those around us. 'Showing that we aren't afraid to laugh about our

---

128 Aaker, Bagdonas, p. 53.
129 Aaker and Bagdonas, p. 43 *passim*.
130 Aaker and Bagdonas, p. 63.
131 As related in Chapter 2 on mindset.
132 Aaker, Bagdonas, p. 149.
133 Aaker, Bagdonas, p. 153.

screw-ups makes others feel safe owning up to theirs.'[134] In the words of Dana Bilky Asher, 'Laughter opens us up again.'[135] By dispelling fear, humour takes away the resulting paralysis. In the words of Professor Steare, 'You can't be afraid when something "tickles" you.' [136]

Researchers Nale Lehmann-Willenbrock and Joseph Allen noted, 'Teams that had humour demonstrated more functional communication and problem-solving behaviours, and performed better as a team.'[137]

'Humor also serves as a coping mechanism and it has been reported that people who see the amusing side of problems are more capable of coping with stress.'[138] This is echoed by Ant Middleton: 'Laughter can be a brilliant antidote to stress and allows you to get a new perspective on your situation. No matter how bleak things seem, see if you can find a way to see the funny side.'[139]

Two of the funniest businessmen I know are Nurul Basher and Saeed Hassan, who, like the brilliant, black, English comedian, Sir Lenny Henry, started using humour at a very early age. Sir Lenny states in an interview after receiving his knighthood, 'I was getting beaten up by racists in the park and I could not

---

134 Aaker, Bagdonas, p. 154.
135 Quoted in Aaker, Bagdonas, p. 154.
136 Interview of 7th August 2021.
137 Quoted in Aaker, Bagdonas, p. 170.
138 https://journals.physiology.org/doi/full/10.1152/advan.00030.2017.
139 Ant Middleton, *Mental Fitness* (Harper Collins, 2021), p. 185.

fight, so I started to say funny things to the racists rather than fighting back. And people used to say, "Leave Lenny alone. Len is all right". I just thought [sic] *if I can make them laugh, it stops them beating me up*, and also it is this thing with people who want to hang out with me.'[140]

My friend Nurul Basher makes the same statement. Being the first Asian pupil in his school, humour enabled him to deal with bullies. He found that his jokes bridged the gap for him. He now uses humour more deliberately in business; he feels it warms people to him and makes him look friendlier.[141]

Saeed Hassan is an eminent corporate lawyer who also started using humour in the school playground.[142] 'It was an appeal for attention and to be liked.' He admits that it helped hide his natural shyness and portray himself as the opposite of his real self. However, whilst he uses humour to differentiate himself from other lawyers, he does not use it with clients. When using humour, you have to be careful as they might not understand, he believes. Making a joke about everyday chores – such as emptying the bins – also helps him get his two daughters to attend to such tedious domestic tasks.

As an international executive, I recognise that some of my jokes fall on deaf ears with non-English listeners. What works

---

140 https://www.irishmirror.ie/showbiz/celebrity-news/lenny-henry-honour-being-knighted-9978978.
141 Interview of 28th August 2021.
142 Interview of 19th August 2021.

in one culture might not work elsewhere. Humour is not a one-stop solution.

For my 'ex', Christopher Harding, humour was a way of looking at things differently. When the Sellafield site of British Nuclear Fuels was named as one of the fastest-growing tourist venues, he quipped that this was not difficult, given that they had not had any visitors the previous year. He would also jest that ducks flying in the region were visible at night because of the radiation. Not necessarily the type of comment that would go down well everywhere, but certainly memorable.

Rita Clifton comments, 'Being funny in a particular way' can help you stand out.[143] As Saeed, the corporate lawyer, puts it, 'Imagine being at an event where you meet a countless number of people. What will differentiate one handshake from another is that they made you laugh.'

'Most humour relies on a shift in dimension, or the creation of a new creation, or the simple surprise that an unexpected ending can happen.' This happened to me once when visiting a very angry client with my colleague, Eric. As the client was ranting and raving about the service he had received, Eric interjected out of the blue, 'What is your favourite restaurant?' Stunned, the client was stopped mid-rant and the meeting went on, but on a more even tone. By using this type of

---

143 Clifton, p. 203.

riposte, 'you're showing others that such remarks don't faze you nearly as much as they would someone else'.[144]

Unerman and Jacob state in their book that humour in women is often surprising and 'can give them the edge.' It cuts through because it is unexpected. It is a 'leveller'[145] Referring to my own sense of humour, Saeed commented that its effectiveness comes from the surprise 'that a well-spoken and well-to-do [sic] woman can have a bawdy sense of humour'.

For me, I would propose that humour is a lot more. Not only is it a 'leveller' but it is also a form of control. By making the status of all parties equal, humour ensures that no one has the upper hand. 'Witty comebacks take the power away from the insult hurled.'[146]

I put this idea to Andrew Tarvin, the US humour expert, who wrote to me in a private exchange, 'As for whether or not humour is a form of control, I suppose it is in a way (or we might call it an *influence technique*). Humour can help you deflect (so controlling a narrative) and it does often increase speaker likability (so influencing people's relationship towards you).'

As Jerry Seinfeld put it, 'People have an infinite attention span if you are entertaining them.'

---

144 Patrick King, *The Art of Witty Banter, Be Quick, Be Clever, Quick & Magnetic* (Amazon, 2022), p. 111.

145 Unerman and Jacob, p. 87.

146 Patrick King, p. 116.

To quote Tarvin again, 'That's because humour improves productivity, reduces stress, prevents burnout, provides motivation, and increases the size of paychecks. It also boosts overall brain power, improves decision-making, increases the acceptance of ideas, triggers new connections, and enhances problem-solving skills.

'One, grabbing people's attention, making sure they actually listen to lessons you have to give. Two, improving understanding, helping connect what you teach with what they already know. And three, practising a skill, giving participants a chance to build proficiency and new capabilities in a way they enjoy.'

I use humour a lot in my English language lessons; it relaxes the student, grabs their attention and enables them to better absorb the data – because data itself is not memorable; it is up to you to make it compelling.

I often used humour/incongruity when dealing with Maxwell. There is no better illustration of this than when I (finally) obtained an appointment with him to discuss the future of Maxwell Satellite. Aware of his short attention span, I created a chart with the name of the other five licence holders and columns referring to the equipment and/or arrangements they had made (satellite uplinks and other related matters). There were ticks against their names in some of the columns, but none in the row relating to our company.

Armed with this chart, I showed Maxwell (who was sitting on his desk, Handy Pandy style, with son Ian behind in the office chair) and then ad-libbed in a Cockney voice, 'And you know what we have Mr Maxwell? We 'ave F**k all!' The change of language totally gripped him and produced the effect I had hoped the chart would – but the chart alone would not have been enough... Using a different form of language/accent helped me make a point.[147]

From then on, he agreed to the sale of the company. Not the resolution I was hoping for, but a resolution nonetheless. The point though here is that my incongruous, vulgar statement uttered in a Cockney accent grabbed Maxwell's attention.

The importance of humour in the workplace is illustrated by Procter & Gamble. When they were looking for a CEO for their Baby, Feminine and Family Care sector, they understandably interviewed several candidates, but what tipped the balance in favour of Fama Francisco was that she had a good sense of humour.

This morning, when crossing a small residential street with my 'walker' (a sort of Zimmer on wheels which I am using while my hip recovers), in front of me, there was a lady in a motorised wheelchair waiting at the intersection. It was a bit like two cowboys facing each other, waiting to see who would give way first. Add to this, two vans were coming in opposite directions that also wanted to cross this tiny street. I decided

---

147 Whitty-Collins a female executive who helped her with her research commented that she leveraged the power of 'deliberate excessive swearing' (p. 135).

to concede defeat and went round her chair with a quip, 'It's a bit of a traffic jam' – to which she retorted in an angry voice, "I can't get through because of the rubbish bags and now have to go in a different direction.' Now, who do you think had the better day after that small incident? I would venture to say it was me, whilst the old lady probably carried on her journey in a grumpy mood.

Patrick King suggests that humour is linked to mindset: 'There's a reason that some people seem to have funny quips every minute ... The difference isn't that they're inherently funnier; it's that they have the right mindset for it. They're prepared for humour, even hunting for it.'

ASK YOURSELF:

Do you ever use humour in the workplace?

Can you think of a time when it worked well?

Are there other instances when you could use humour?

CHAPTER 12

THE PERCEPTION OF WOMEN IN THE WORKPLACE – AND WHAT MEN AND WOMEN CAN LEARN FROM EACH OTHER

Living in Central London as I do, when I think about men, I often think of the Gentlemen's Club – and, in the context of business, how men congregate with each other and support each other – not just in the workplace but in their leisure time as well – whether it is over a game of football or on the golf course. Women have yet to learn this.

As Gill Whitty-Collins, so aptly puts it: 'Sisters are (not) doing it for themselves'.[148] As if to emphasise my jokey comment about needing a Kevlar vest when dealing with other female executives, she goes on to explain that 'men see this lack of support [...] and they comment on it, saying that women are [...] "too jealous and threatened to support each other".'

Gill Whitty-Collins mentions another contributory factor; more women need to come forward as mentors, as 'men who do mentor women can't offer much in the way of psychological support – how to deal with sexism, for instance'.

---

148 Whitty-Collins, p.145.

The mentorship need not restrict itself to the business sector either. Cancer Research has launched an excellent initiative to allow female executives like myself to mentor female research scientists. It is called Women of Influence and, in my case, I have been paired with the lovely Yin Yin, a native Chinese lady with a PhD in algorithms (no less!).

The other key strategy women have to learn from men is that of ASKING. I have talked about the power of the ASK at great length when discussing various aspects of communications, but the fact remains that men are more likely to negotiate a rise than their female counterparts. I sincerely hope that the tips in this book will help 'the fair sex' drop their 'fairness' in favour of a more assertive style.

What can men learn from women?

There are many social skills that men can impart to women, but – as was pointed out to me by a male colleague – women can also share some of their natural talents with their male counterparts. If only to underline how unbiased I am, I am quoting the following insights from Mike Michalowicz:[149]

1. **Work/home balance:** 'Women typically strive to find a balance between the frequently competing demands of work and home. They may not do it perfectly; the balance may shift from time to time, and

---

149 https://www.americanexpress.com/en-us/business/trends-and-insights/articles/8-traits-every-male-leader-needs-to-learn-from-women/

they may sacrifice sleep to try to be a good worker/
partner/mother, but the important lesson here is that
it's important to try – to recognize that both work and
home are important and deserve our attention. Men
can miss out on important events and demands at
home in favour of a single-minded focus on business
tasks. However, in focusing primarily on work, men
can lose out on the valuable support and fulfilment
derived from spending time and effort nurturing life
outside of work.'

2. **Efficient multi-tasking:** Enough has been written
   about this in both serious works and comic sketches
   to spare you any more on the subject!

3. **Making presentation matter:** 'Women know this
   because, whether or not it's fair, for generations
   they've been evaluated based on their appearance
   more than men have. While it's always been true that
   appearances matter, given that the average attention
   span is getting increasingly shorter, first impressions
   are more important than ever. You have one shot to
   look pulled together, organized and capable at first
   glance. Don't waste that opportunity – look your best.'

4. **Modesty calling out for help! – Broadcast your
   spot of bother!:** We joke about men who are
   unwilling to ask for directions, but there's no shame in
   finding the expert on a topic and asking for a tutorial.
   Take your smartphone as one example. Chances are

good that you've installed an app in the past month or two, but how well do you really know how to use it? There's something to be said for taking a few minutes to watch a tutorial or ask tech support for help. Use your resources!

5. **Farming rather than hunting:** Historically, men have been the hunters, whilst women have been the gatherers and community builders. It all goes back to the Stone Age when man were the hunter-gatherers providing food for the family and woman stayed at home tended to the farming and, generally 'cultivating' their world.

6. **Collaboration:** Business moves quicker today than it ever has before and it's increasingly specialised. No man is an island, and while I may have to remind myself of that every now and then, women embrace that concept more readily. So, work with your team by seeking out the experts among your staff to complete tasks that you may struggle with. Your company will function better as a team than as adversaries.

This has not always been the case. As Sandberg puts it, 'One of the obstacles to more women gaining power has sometimes been women already in power... They often viewed each other as competition. In more than one interview, I have even joked that I had to wear a Kevlar, for fear of being stabbed in the back by one of my female colleagues.'[150]

Nicholas D. Kristof sums it up beautifully in his 2012 article in *The New York Times*. The title is 'Women Hurting Women'.[151]

This is less so nowadays with the advent of The Sisterhood by the founder of The Allbright, Debbie Wosskow OBE and Anna Jones, as well The Women in Business Club, set up by Raimonda Jan.

There is also another point on which Mike and I do not totally agree:

7. **Social skills**. He states, 'Women excel at networking and using social media to support their connections, both personal and business. Take a lesson from their willingness to share and communicate freely.' Whilst my female counterparts may be good at publicising the fashion they are wearing or the products they endorse, direct, old fashioned face-to-face networking remains to me a domain in which men excel – whether by rugby trips, golf weekends or nights out on the town.

Furthermore, if you are in a corporate, legal or, say, banking profession, there is nothing to substitute relationships based

---

150 Sandberg, Chapter 11, p. 164.

151 https://www.nytimes.com/2012/09/30/opinion/sunday/kristof-women-hurting-women.html

on trust, respect and personal interaction, and men still outshine women in this respect.

Women's collaborative approach to management is also an attribute that results in better management; whereas 'the male bias is reflected in the false conception of leadership as mere command and control'.[152]

More recently, a plethora of publications have defended how women score better over men[153]; EQ is much cited here.[154] Self-control and greater risk aversion are also evoked, making banks with women in senior positions 'more resilient to the financial crisis'.[155] 'Extensive research has linked gender differences in aggressiveness to testosterone, which is systematically higher in men than women.' And, as if Premuzic was defending my contention that both sexes can benefit from each other, 'Exposing men to women inhibits their testosterone bursts, making men less aggressive and helping them delay gratification.'[156]

If there is one area in which women have the upper hand, it is in the realm of emotions; women are much more open emotionally, whereas men have to conform to the need of

---

152 James MacGregor Burns, quoted in *Women Don't Ask, Linda Babcock and Sara Laschever* (Princeton University Press, 2021), p. 179.
153 Premuzic, pp. 86 onwards.
  Harvard Business Review ....
154 D. Goleman.
155 Premuzic, p. 97, 98.
156 Premuzic, p. 99.

being seen to be strong. If you are unsure about this utterance, I would point you to the high percentage of male suicides.[157]

In their excellent paper on *Women and The Vision Thing*,[158] Herminia Ibarra and Otilia Obaduru contend that female executives are not as visionary as their male counterparts. I dare say that this is probably correct, and probably due to the fact that, as mentioned earlier, women are much more detail-oriented than men. This attention to minutiae is a strength in execution, but a weakness in seeing the bigger picture. Raimonda Jan comments that men build their parachute on the way down. Women think about how they are going to build their parachute. This no doubt comes from the way in which we are brought up. 'Parents treat girls more gingerly while allowing boys more latitude around adventure seeking.'[159]

As Margaret Thatcher put it, 'If you want anything said, ask a man. If you want anything done, ask a woman.'

As well as being risk averse, women are also paralysed by their wish to be polite and are blighted by the old adage 'speak only when spoken to'. Whitty-Collins goes even further: she asserts that women do not perform as well as men in Zoom/Team Video calls, as they are unable to get a word in edgeways.[160]

---

157 See my blog …

158 *On Women and Leadership* (HBR's 10 Must Reads, 2019), p. 81.

159 V Young, p. 224.

160 Whitty-Collins, p. 103.

She further argues that women believe in MERITOCRACY, but many places are non-meritocratic.[161] The irony there does not escape me, as meritocracy is often seen to favour men over women... a subject for another time.

I would like to concentrate for a minute (or two!) on assertiveness versus aggression. The main difference, for me, lies in the fact that aggression is linked to emotion, whilst assertiveness is a function of logic and behaviour. Chase Hill says it best: 'Assertiveness is the ability to stand up for yourself or other people in a calm, positive way without being aggressive or upsetting others. Assertive people express their thoughts and feelings in an appropriate and respectful manner.'[162] Throughout my career, I have done my best to stay on the side of assertiveness by being polite and respectful of other people's feelings. I am told I have succeeded and I hope that I can honestly say that the fact that I have not made any enemies in my career is an indicator that I have managed to negotiate that tightrope.

The divergent perception of women in the workplace is perhaps best illustrated by the nicknames attributed to female executives. We all know of Mrs Thatcher's 'Iron Lady'; 'Ice Maiden'. Mine was 'The Dish' – which I honestly can deal with; it was apparently a pun on my being the CEO of a satellite communication company ('dish' as in 'satellite dish' – get it?) and a comment on my outward appearance.

---

161 Whitty-Collins, p. 119.

162 Chase Hill, *Assertive Communication Skills* (Amazon, 2021), p. 15.

But the one that, to this day, completely shocks me is the attribution of 'Chick with a dick' to Karen Espley, who undertook a trip to Antarctica sponsored by Standard Life.

The gracious Sam Tulloch,[163] business change and transformation consultant and project manager, pointed out an additional complexity to male vs female work relationships – that of being the sole black person and woman in an IT environment. She explained to me that she often goes into what is called 'code switching', which I understand to mean, in this context, as changing from one *type* of language to another.[164]

She takes on a stance of humility, downplaying her intelligence and knowledge, starting her statement with a comment such as 'I am not a techie.' Sam, who is extremely concerned to maintain assertiveness without being aggressive, only resorts to 'masculine behaviour' as a last resort. So, I pose a question here: Might it help men to tone down their confident behaviour in some circumstances?

---

163 Interview of 24/1/2022.
164 Rather than the more conventional meaning of switching from one language to another...

ASK YOURSELF:

Do you believe you can learn from the opposite gender and vice-versa?

List here what you think you could learn.

CHAPTER 13

SETTING BOUNDARIES

Boundaries are not about keeping people out, but about people communicating with better clarity and maintaining one another's values and needs. By setting boundaries with your colleagues, you are telling them what works for/with you and what does not; you are defining how far they can go and – also – where not to go.

As James Smith often does, he points out the obvious and uncomplicates the subject of boundaries:

'Boundaries never physically exist unless we build them; even the boundaries between countries, states, counties and cities are made up and do not physically exist, so the ones in your mind are even less real.'[165]

For too long, I have been all too willing to help people out – even if it meant my giving up an activity or somehow complicating my life. It has taken me years to realise that I should curb my eagerness to please/come to the rescue. Not only was this volunteering impacting my work and leisure

---

165 James Smith, *NOT A Life Coach* (Harper Collins Publishers, 2020), p. 87.

time, but it often was also not helping the person in question; what they often REALLY needed was to find a solution for themselves, rather than assistance from the likes of me.

Boundaries are about saying 'no' and not feeling guilty. However, boundaries only become valid if you realise you have choices; you do not HAVE to be available 24 hours a day.

Sharon Martin explains that boundaries are set in three steps:

1) Identify your boundaries. Be clear on what you need before trying to communicate or enforce the boundary.

2) Communicate your boundaries or expectations clearly, calmly, and consistently. Stick to the facts without overexplaining, blaming, or becoming defensive.

3) If your boundaries aren't respected, evaluate your options and take action.[166]

Realise that boundaries are different for everybody; the onus is on YOU to make it clear what YOUR preferences are. 'Setting boundaries with co-workers can also help to prevent conflicts before they happen.'[167]

---

166 https://www.livewellwithsharonmartin.com/set-boundaries-toxic-people/

167 Dr Henry Mark, *Positive Boundaries at Workplace* (Amazon, 2021).

How do you know when you need to set up boundaries? When:

► You feel that your job consists of responding to other people's messages and calls (see Simon case study below).

► You feel you have lost control of your time and are spending too much of it dealing with other people's needs.

► You feel your colleagues are taking advantage of you.

► You are trying to help in matters which are beyond your control.

My friend, Simon, came to visit me recently, bearing a stiff neck and asking for advice. Aged thirty-four, he had recently become a father for the first time and was sharing all the domestic and parental duties with his wife, Caroline. They developed a plan whereby she would attend to their lovely baby son, Jared, between 08.00 to 18.00 on weekdays and sometimes weekends as well. This enabled Simon, who worked from home, to have uninterrupted time with his work. However, he was not able to switch off from work matters after 18.00 and, as much as he loved his son, he would still regularly consult his phone and felt obliged to reply before going to bed. Simon recognised that his clients did not expect a reply out of hours, but HE had this compulsion to reply there and then.

He was angry with himself for not being able to give Caroline and Jared his undivided attention and felt he was also neglecting his own father. Simon recognised that the problem was with him, but did not know how to change things.

It was not the first time I had heard a client torn between work and family. When I saw how relieved Simon was to hear that he was not alone with this dilemma, I decided to relate this story to him, without revealing the person's identity. So, picture this: a father drives back from work and parks outside the house, armed with a briefcase in one hand, a phone in the other, only to be assailed (in his view) by his children running up to him, wanting to hug him and attract his attention. With his hands full, he was unable to return their hugs and also felt a little overwhelmed by their welcome.

Simon's predicament reminded me of one of my tutor's experiences, Professor Damian Hughes. I determined with this client that the best way to change things was by changing *his* behaviour, not his children's – and even more, his mindset. We developed a new routine for him: he would stop the car one block or so away from the house and place any last work-related phone calls. He would then get out and put both the phone and the briefcase into the boot of his car, drive home and park outside, as before. The difference was that he now entered the family dwelling empty-handed and could return his children's urgent embraces. Simple, you might say – and you may be right: who wants changes to be laborious and painful?

Now, getting back to Simon... This anecdote got him thinking; it showed him that he might be able to resolve his work/home dilemma by (only) changing his behaviour. In less than an hour, we developed a new work pattern. It turned out that Simon had a room in the house that was allocated to him as his 'office'. Realising that he would want to remain contactable by his nearest and dearest, I suggested that he might like to buy a second (cheap) phone which would have a number known only to his inner circle when they wished to reach him after 18.00. He was to leave his existing phone in the office and carry on the rest of the evening without any work-related messages/requests. He could now commit his time and his mind totally to his family, without any feelings of guilt.

This strategy so appealed to Simon that the neck pain he'd had on arrival had disappeared; in fact, he stated with glee that he felt as if a load had been taken off his shoulders. But the plan was not over yet; we now had to look at *how* to implement it (otherwise, a plan is only a plan...). As it turns out, Simon had a redundant phone he could use for the evening calls, so all he had to do (but it was still a task to be completed), was to enter into a contract with the cheapest mobile phone provider. To add accountability to this new undertaking, I asked him to email me when he had made that arrangement. But, there was still another matter – and that was adjusting his clients' expectations. They had become used to Simon responding to their messages/emails within a very short time. Putting this new plan into action, Simon had to explain to his audience that he had set up amended working hours of 09.00 to 18.00

and that after-hour interactions would not be dealt with until 09.00 the next working day.

Simon's case highlights another issue. In the same way that we talked about saying 'no' to others, the same holds true for saying 'no' to yourself. Only, here, it is depriving yourself of what you want.

Many years ago, one of my colleagues was asked what I was like as a boss. His response was 'tough but fair'. The problem is that no one is tougher on me than myself. As it is, I am presently working with a charming female executive, Sylvia, who is a perfectionist in her job and always delivers excellent results. As I have followed her over several years (in three different jobs), I have been able to identify a recurring trend: taking on board whatever requests are put her way; an inability to ask for extra help and a total disregard for her own personal welfare. The problem, in other words, is not with her employers or the job; it is about her relationship with herself.

Over time, I have been able to help her realise that looking after herself is a good thing and that it means that what she needs to change is her relationship with herself and her needs. The change will come from within.

Top of the list: holidays. It is no accident that holidays are also referred to as 'taking a break' – stepping away from the current situation and 'taking stock'. I should know! I fell into the trap of not taking breaks during my time at Institutional Investor, even though my motivation was different. I wanted to demonstrate my loyalty to the company by staying 'on the job' and not taking time off for three consecutive years! Of course, this self-sacrifice made absolutely no impact and, if in anything, probably pointed to a weakness – my inability to take my needs into account.

Going back to Sylvia; once she had set her mind to take time off, she self-sabotaged the project by looking at destinations and then sorting out dates. I suggested that she might like to consider first choosing dates according to work schedules and then selecting the location. By doing things in this order, she would ensure that the preferred time would enable her to truly relax and not concern herself about what she might be 'missing'. In short, she was learning to put herself first.

It is impossible to touch on boundaries without talking about assertiveness, which – in turn – 'helps improve one's sense of self-worth'.[168] Turnbull goes on to quote Daniel Ames[169] and underlines how balancing high and low assertiveness at work is crucial for efficiency and productivity. Low assertiveness can lead to imposter syndrome, whilst high assertiveness can come across as bullying.

Analysing what is important to you can help you better understand your values, principles and goals. You are one step closer to defining the boundaries you need to put into place. Keep in mind that you have a choice and can always

---

168 Turnbull, p. 17.
169 Turnbull, p. 32.

say 'no'. Make your refusal clear; do not dilute it with a lot of explanations or apologies.

Putting yourself first is not necessarily an act of selfishness. Think about what happens in the event of a plane crash: you are instructed to put your oxygen mask on first. The reason? If you lose consciousness, you can't help anyone around you.

By the same token, you need to become aware of what you can and are willing to do.[170] Failing to do so can result in burnout.

ASK YOURSELF:

Is there a situation at work or at home where a change of behaviour will help you?

What is it?

How can you change the behaviour?

---

170 Turnbull, p. 40.

CHAPTER 14

CONFIDENCE IS NOT ARROGANCE

I have long been fascinated by the difference between arrogance and assertiveness.

I am happy to confess that I have shown confidence throughout a great part of my life, but I am told that this never came through as arrogance. One of my closest and most long-standing friends, Susan S., says that I was always 'self-possessed' and that my humour dispelled any hint of arrogance.

Keeping emotion out of the message is indeed a key factor towards better communication of an idea, but the main issue is that women still strive too much for 'likeability'.[171] This prevents female executives from raising their voices. In my view, women whinge far too much, about not 'being heard'. If you have something to say, get on and say it! And do not let your emotions dilute your message. With age, my confidence has grown – I am no longer worried about my 'likeability'.

---

171 Whitty- Collins, p. 156-7.

Confidence can be gained in steps, as is illustrated in Hill's 21-day training programme.[172]

Confidence comes from within and 'should never rest on the approval of others. Just as, importantly, you should never judge yourself in comparison to others... Your fragile external confidence is like a paper house that can disappear at the slightest puff of wind. The solution is to build a core of internal self-confidence that you can call on when times get tough.'[173] 'Your confidence should be based on what you know you're capable of, not the opinion of others.'[174] In other words, do not waste your time comparing yourself to others – be authentic to yourself.

Tear yourself away from self-esteem to self-worth. Realise that you are a work in progress and that you are okay at all times. You may have lost the big deal – and of course, that may cause a whole host of consequences – but, by refocusing on your inner self-worth ('I'm still okay; I'm a work in progress; I did the best that I could with the resources available to me and I will take the learnings into the next situation'), you can limit the personal damage that a challenging situation may have over you.[175]

---

172 Chase Hill, p. 162 *passim*.

173 A Middleton, *Mental Fitness,* p. 32-3.

174 A Middleton, *Mental Fitness,* p. 51.

175 With thanks to my former tutor, John Perry.

I like Whitty-Collins' definition of confidence as 'a degree of certainty and an absence of doubt'.[176]

Here are my five points for establishing your self-confidence:

1. Learn to speak to yourself as you would to your best friend – showing the same compassion and lack of judgement.

2. Accept that getting self-confidence may not happen overnight and, where necessary, use tools, such as a change of posture and attention to what you wear – to meet your goal.

3. Avoid procrastination; accept you will never achieve perfection. Triple-checking data serves no real purpose.

4. Create boundaries and stick to them!

5. Overcome your fear of speaking out. As in the Nike slogan, 'Just Do It!' Seize the moment – it may never come again!

Once you have accepted that you are a work in progress, allow yourself to use some of the tools we have mentioned in this book. Do not get me wrong, I am not proposing that you 'fake it 'til you make it', but shield your vulnerability.

---

176 Whitty-Collins, p. 88.

For instance, dressing for success can be a good start. No surprise that a successful woman like Dame Cilla Snowball, the former group chairman and group CEO at AMV BBDO, Governor of Wellcome Trust and Director of Genome Research Limited, as well as Derwent Ltd, talks about 'armour' when referring to her dress code in some instances.[177] However, ensure that your dress code is authentic – remember, it is widely accepted that one of the reasons Hilary Clinton's campaign for the presidency failed is because she adopted a very masculine look (trousers and jacket), which did not fit her character.

For me, my major coat of armour is unquestionably humour. I hide behind a clown's mask. In reality, behind my buffoonery is a very serious person. Humour often helps me to make a point with a firmness that would not occur in normal speech. When networking, humour also allows me to be more memorable. Too often, people do not remember WHAT you said, but they do recall HOW they felt. If you made them laugh, they will more readily recall the meeting. Humour can also relieve tension in the air – taking the conversation to another level.

Procrastination is the tell-sign of low self-confidence and, by eliminating it, you will also enhance your confidence – to yourself and the outside world. In this respect, I am quite lucky in that I rarely put things off. No surprise, therefore, that my friends say that my middle initial 'A' (as in Catherine Anne Baudino) refers to Action Woman. I have, if you like, a 'Go for

---

177 Whitty-Collins, p. 139.

it!' approach to any given situation. This Action-Mode (as I call it) demonstrates itself in the most trivial ways. Only yesterday, tickets were released for an event some dear friends and I were keen to attend; I dropped everything and proceeded to secure the necessary places for us.

Women seem to have an innate desire to display perfection but we are human; we make mistakes. This unreasonable need translates itself into countless revisions and further research, which is followed by even more research, 'in case something has been left out'. Accept that something will always be omitted and you must call it a day before you put forward your argument! I admit here that, as much as I am Action Woman, I have revised the draft of this book far too many times and have delayed putting in the final full stop! Whilst I have jokingly referred to my manuscript as my *opus maximus*,[178] I have had to curb my desire to reach perfection. How have I done that? You might ask. Well, in my case, being accountable to my writing coach, the gorgeous (but sometimes formidable) Georgia Varjas, herself a three-time author. Another method might be to set yourself a time limit for your task.

Boundaries are unquestionably the ultimate weapon, not only in self-survival but also in gaining respect from those around you. Just as you might surround yourself in battle with appropriate protection, so too in the corporate jungle you should establish no-go areas. You give yourself space to think and act as required in the given environment.

---

178 Latin for my 'major work".

The establishment of boundaries also prevents you from falling into what I coin 'the likeability trap' and ignoring your needs in favour of others.

Young lists what she calls your 'List of Rights' – 20 in total[179] – of which my favourite is the right to say 'no' without feeling guilty.

Speaking out is undoubtedly an act of courage. The failure to speak out implies consent at the very least. Here, I would like to dwell further on female executives ranting over the need to have their 'voice' heard. Aged sixteen, I literally lost my voice when my father had a heart attack and had to be hospitalised at the then-St George's Hospital on Hyde Park Corner (now the Landsdowne Hotel). That did not stop me from sitting the first (written) part of the *Baccalauréat* and obtaining the best mark, not only at The French Lycée in London but also the whole *Académie de Lille* – which was the governing body.[180]

To those female executives who complain that their voice is not being heard, I would ask 'What is stopping you from speaking out?' We all know that silence equals acceptance, not to mention capitulation. So, I implore you: Raise your voice, ASK! Arm yourself with self-worth and GO FORTH! Do not stop yourself from being a disrupter. You are blessed with a voice; USE IT!

---

179 V Young, pp. 249-250
180 My voice unexpectedly came back the next day.

I admit that my upbringing has made me resilient and somewhat fearless but if I have reached that level of courage, what is stopping you?

For male readers: The early games you played as a child have formed you (as they formed most women). Boys play war games in which they 'die' and then pick themselves up to 'live' another day whilst girls play with their dolls in a quiet corner and hone their nurturing talents. I would invite you to reconsider some basic gender biases. It is certainly true that women need to curb their emotional outbursts in the workplace, but it is equally true that they need to review their reactions to these outpourings. As Brescoll puts it, 'When women express [emotions] at work... they can be seen as out of control... it is almost expected for men to get angry... a man who gets angry at work may well be admired for it.'[181]

I would go even further: ensure your work environment is a safe place where a woman can learn from a man as much as a man can learn from his female counterpart. When you spot a time when she runs the risk of being seen as 'arrogant', rather than 'assertive', take her aside and discuss an alternative approach. That requires courage and tact on your part, but what satisfaction to help a colleague! If that is still too much for you, ask another woman to discuss the matter with her.

---

181 Brescoll, VL, 2011, *Who Takes The Floor and Why* (Administrative, Science Quarterly, Vol. 56, No 4).

Speaking of confidence – do not be intimidated by people's titles but, of course, stay within the boundaries of civility. Manners are really important to me and were ingrained into me as a child. I am not talking about Debrett's code of etiquette, but about respect. For a few years, I sat on the fundraising committee for The Royal Engineers Museum in Chatham, alongside corporate and army grandees such as Sir David McAlpine, Sir this and Sir that AND General Sir George Cooper, who was no less than the head of The Royal Engineers and bore the title of Chief Royal Engineer. I was intrigued by how these eminent businessmen, who were often millionaires, would defer to George and still called him SIR. As for me? Well, I called him 'George Darling', which amused him no end. He was so used to being recognised for his title, that he was tickled pink to be recognised as a human being. Not only was I the youngest on this committee, but I was also the only female amongst these distinguished men.

There is a further point I wish to address in the realm of confidence – how we accept rejection and/or criticism. Again, in this type of circumstance, women take negative statements much more personally than men. Psychologists argue that boys' military games of kill-and-be-killed explain male resilience to negative feedback. The expression 'water off a duck's back' comes to mind.

In such instances, whether a man or a woman, I would invite you to consider the criticism as being addressed to your message/ thought/idea and not to you *personally.* I remember in my youth taking criticism as proof that people did not 'like me', but it had nothing to do with my likeability at all. By dropping your self-esteem and reinforcing your self-worth, you will be able to see things more clearly and rationally!

Titles certainly play a part in confidence but beware of any deluges of grandeur attached to them! Having a job title can be a shortcut to more effective leadership for the following reasons:

Internal reasons – referring to the lift incident at Maxwell's Empire, it was important for the staff of this recently acquired company to understand that I was there as both their ambassador and as the representative of their new owner, the media tycoon.

External reasons – titles are an insidious part of society. Whether we like it or not, we are defined from the minute we are born by a title. Say, Mr, Master, Miss, Ms, Sir, Lady, The Right Hon., etc. In this respect, females have the worst end of the stick as their name often denominates their marital status. No wonder more and more have adopted the term 'Ms'! I consider myself very lucky to be able to answer to 'Dr Baudino.'

I also never took up my husband's surname, partly due to my more rebellious streak, but also for practical reasons. When we married, I was thriving in an international career where secretaries knew me as Dr Baudino. Changing my name would have involved confusion and a prolonged explanation in a foreign language – just to get in touch with their boss.

There was one instance, though, during one of Alastair's 'disappearances', where the wonderful, charitable Samaritans called me, addressing me as 'Mrs Garrow.' My reaction was not exactly a charitable one – I recall shouting 'I am not Mrs Garrow and have never been! Thank God!' It was no doubt a reaction to my hurt at what was undoubtedly another suicide attempt, but it was certainly not very nice of me – but telling, nonetheless.

I remain very proud of my title as 'Dr' and will always recall defending my PhD thesis in front of my supervisor and an examiner. It is an oral exam in which you have to prove your work is genuine and authentically yours. Once the examiners felt they had covered all the relevant points, they asked me to step out of the room and wait outside. After what seemed like an eternity, my supervisor came out and said, 'Would you like to come back in, Dr Baudino?' Yippee! I had passed...

As for job titles, ah, there is an interesting one! My first lesson to you is not to let it go to your head. You are only as good as the time you bear the label of CEO, Head of ..., whatever! Once that title goes, so do the flowers, bottles of wine, invitations to Ascot, etc.

Perhaps even more ironic, the converse is also true.

For several years, I was an unpaid board member of the French Chamber of Commerce in the UK. I also founded and chaired the Franco-British Construction Industry Group and created an alliance with the RICS (The Royal Institution of Chartered

Surveyors). This last initiative led to a joint publication called *The Business of Building in France*. All new territory for the Chamber and ones that gave our Group much credibility.

The creation of this new business group proved to be a big earner for the Chamber, which relied on memberships and events to supplement the French government's meagre support. I am pleased to say that such was my contribution to the Chamber's coffers that they held a cocktail party in my honour. This little celebration went by without so much as a comment from the president of the Chamber – the head of one of the French investment banks. However, that all changed when I was subsequently appointed as the first European business director of the NASDAQ stock market. The said individual went out of his way to make contact – to the point that he'd now decided to address me in the more familiar *'tu'* form. Clearly, in his mind, by being appointed to NASDAQ, I had achieved far more than in my voluntary and money-making contribution to the very Chamber he chaired...

Do not let your title go to your head!

ASK YOURSELF:

Are you frightened of coming across as arrogant?

Is there someone you can sound this out with? It might be someone you admire in your environment. Consider reaching out to them for help. Work out here how you will approach the subject.

CHAPTER 15

Travelling Tips for the Lone Lady

Perhaps you are recently divorced or widowed. The children have flown the coop. The holiday season beckons; your friends are all busy with their families and you are reluctant to go away alone.

You are too mature to envisage student hostels, let alone back-packing, although I do recognise that hostels are a good way to meet other solo travellers. I prefer to immerse myself in the local culture. It is also for this reason that I avoid sea cruises or themed holidays. So, when I say I travel solo, I mean 'solo'.

Many friends of mine think I am brave to travel solo. I am not brave at all; I am an experienced voyager – for both business and pleasure and I have developed some useful tips and habits.

I spent my first holiday abroad in a hotel, on my own, aged seventeen. I stayed in a three-star hotel in the centre of Paris and walked everywhere from there on foot for a week. I took myself out for a boiled egg in a café at lunchtime and out for dinner somewhere close by if my Parisian relatives were busy. So, I am an early hand at solo travelling and, at the same time, I am not ashamed to say that it was not back-packing. My personal safety and comfort have always remained a prime consideration on all of my outings.

My perfect holiday consists, in general, of a mixture of sun and culture. A sunny destination is not enough on its own; there need to be some interesting places to visit. This does not suit everyone and my budget may not fit everyone's purse either, so I often travel alone. Only one other friend in my circle of friends travels solo without the pretext of a theme (golf, wine tasting, etc.). The fact that my travel choices do not match everyone's taste or wallet will not stop me from setting off with my passport in hand.

Chase Hill highlights a feature of travelling alone that may not occur to all of us: 'Travelling alone allows you learn [sic] about yourself on a different scale because you are in various locations and, hopefully, diverse cultures.'[182] He continues to argue that solo travel also gives you time to assess your needs. I would add that you do need an amount of self-confidence to travel alone; you need to be comfortable with yourself.

But, before dwelling on tips and comments, I would like to explain to one and all the reason why I am focusing on the solo traveller and that is because singletons are not treated equally in the hospitality business. It is a sector I particularly appreciate, but I have to recognise that it is not uncommon for a single traveller to be relegated to a table close to the kitchen or worse... toilets – where you have the opportunity to relish all the smells emanating through the swinging doors.

---

182 Chase Hill, *Assertive Communications Skills,* p. 232.

As for visiting a bar; this is even more problematic for the sole female traveller.

If you are unsure about this premise, I would point to a conversation I recently had with a transexual; she commented how differently she was treated when dressed as a man and how she felt extremely vulnerable when dressed as a woman; the difference in men's behaviour changed from the moment she was standing outside the hotel, waiting for a taxi. Entering a bar on her own made her feel so uncomfortable that she decided not to repeat the experience. These were things she had never thought of before!

1. Research:

For me, it is not just about the destination, but also the journey! I LOVE reading maps (you know, those old paper things which were invented way before Google Maps came into being?). And, when they exist, I like to read updated travel guides. But, I admit, I do not always trust some internet sites such as TripAdvisor. Also, research should cover the layout of the town or district you are in; a traveller armed with a street map is a clear signal of a tourist.

2. The concierge is your best friend:

He/she will be able to give you the best advice for your bookings, tours, etc. Remember their name and let them get to know you.

I even go, sometimes, a step further. Six years ago, I was visiting Miami Beach for the first time and wanted to make the most of my stay. Whilst still in London, I found out the name and email address of the concierge at my hotel, the Eden Roc in Miami South Beach: the divine Joseph Colon. Via the internet, we agreed on which restaurants I should frequent in the evening. I asked him to book these for me.

Such is the relationship that developed between us, Jo and I are still friends on Facebook!

Equally, now returning to Miami, I have put into place the research mentioned here under Point 1. But, unfortunately, there are no handbooks published since my last stay and I cannot believe that Miami has not moved on. So, I have managed to reach out to sets of friends who are based in Miami and have, this time, decided to stay in Downtown Miami; ultimately, I have chosen my hotel on Biscayne Bay on the basis that their video gives a prominent spot to (you guessed it!) their concierge!

3.   In the hotel:

Start the day with enthusiasm – go down for breakfast! Smile at the other guests, and say hello to the ones you come across on the stairs or in the lifts.

If you speak a second language, address them in their language – no matter what level of fluency you have! Compliment people on their dress or their children's behaviour. Engage!

After my first two-week stay at The Dusit Thani Laguna in Phuket, I knew nearly everyone in the hotel – and those I did not know would come to my breakfast table – curious as to why I was the only singleton in the hotel but was talking to so many strangers.

4. Boundaries:

As a solo traveller, you may be approached by fellow voyagers – but need to respect their boundaries. There is nothing worse than a sticky person tagging on. When addressing a married couple, do not limit your comments/words to the husband; be sure to include the wife as well – and vice-versa.

By the same token, establish your boundaries by (say) bringing a notebook with you in which you jot down your thoughts, experiences and even, perhaps, self-discoveries.

My personal boundary setter is also my passport to visit bars and restaurants: a book! My friends quip about 'Baudino and her Book' – and it is quite true. A form of reading is never far away from me. For instance, I do not let the fact that I am solo stop me from visiting the hotel bar – but I do not place myself on a barstool (which might send different messages). Instead, I sit at a table with my drink and ... my novel!

You might say that my book is my tacit signal that I do not want to be disturbed – for instance, if I find myself the recipient of unwanted attention, I just stick my nose back into my book...

5. Going out for dinner:

Again, there is no need to stay in your room in the evening! You are in a different city/location; explore and enjoy! Hotels are pretty much the same wherever you are in the world – remind yourself you're in New York, Vienna – wherever.

Ask your concierge to book your table. This will ensure that you are not seated next to the toilet or the kitchen! The restaurant will also recognise that you are staying in a nice hotel and you should be treated accordingly.

When you walk in, hold your head up high and do not be shy about asking for a better table (if required). Think about what we said earlier on making an impression when walking into a room. And, as well as posture, consider dress.

During a visit to Thailand, I visited a Lady Boy Club. As is the custom in Phuket, the club sent a taxi to pick me up alongside other residents of the hotel. As it is, I shared the car with a somewhat inebriated man with his two 'girlfriends'. When we arrived, the maître d' understandably assumed I was with that party. I quickly explained to her that I did not wish to sit – under any circumstances – with those people. She took it on board and I ended up sitting with the owner and his friends and had a most riveting evening with French, English and Americans.

6. Excursions:

Again, ask your concierge which are the best excursions to go on. Some excursions may boast a lovely boat ride, but neglect to advise you that it will involve a two-hour car journey each way to the pier! Or the seas might be exceptionally choppy on that day.

When on the excursion, you have the opportunity to chat with other travellers – some of whom will be staying in different hotels. Use the shared experience to initiate conversation.

7. Some ice breakers:

Remembering to smile, you might like to enquire:

> ► How long have you been in this hotel/on this holiday?
> ► Have you been here before?
> ► Are there any restaurants you would recommend?
> ► Which excursions should I go on?
> ► Where are you from?

And, as in networking, take an interest in their answers.

8. Practice:

You may like to practice going out by taking yourself out for lunch in a restaurant near you and trying out these techniques prior to your holiday. Otherwise, you may prefer to try out 'themed' holidays around golf, tennis, or cultural visits, building up your self-confidence and 'techniques' along the way.

River cruises also provide a transitional entry into solo travelling. By following the same itinerary, you have ready-made ice-breakers for new exchanges. As my friend, Jenny

Cookman, who is a travel consultant and river cruise specialist, puts it, 'One of the lovely things about travelling solo on a river cruise is that you immediately have something in common with your fellow passengers. Shared experiences give so many opportunities for interesting conversations and making new friends.'

The much more adventurous Karen Espley (who travelled to Antarctica) travelled for three to four years in Australia and New Zealand in a camper van[183] and agrees with my tips, adding five other comments:

- ► Have a plan
- ► Travel light (something I am incapable of!)
- ► Just Do It!
- ► Write a blog – I write pieces called 'Reflexions From ...'
- ► Go out and have fun!

Remember one thing: as in coaching, the journey should be as enjoyable as the destination!

ASK YOURSELF:

What further tips could you offer the solo traveller?

---

183 Zoom interview of 11/1/22.

CHAPTER 16

Dealing with my mortality and possible suffering.
DON'T LET AGE DEFINE YOU

In the course of the last few years, I have had several falls. The worst have resulted in two consecutive fractures to the tibias in each leg, followed by a dual fracture to my right hip.

These unfortunate accidents were peppered with a few more. Ultimately, I was referred to a lovely (Japanese) female doctor at Chelsea & Westminster Hospital, who carried out several tests – including a brain scan. The last one indicated that I had an early onset of dementia – either Alzheimer's or frontal lobe dementia.

More tests will have to be carried out to clarify which. Either way, I have witnessed my delightful and highly intelligent mother-in-law physically and mentally disintegrate with Alzheimer's. My father, on the other hand, had all the character changes and absent-mindedness of frontal lobe dementia – so much so that we had to cut off the gas oven and hob, as he would leave those on for hours at a time.

So here I am in a quandary; what do I do? This is truly the biggest challenge of my life. I – who have gladly assumed the moniker of Action Woman, attributed to me by close friends and colleagues – am now paralysed by the news. The loss of mobility due to the fractures was one thing, but a failing brain function may now be on the cards. After the doctor gave me her preliminary diagnosis, I asked, 'Will I be able to continue practising as a coach?' She replied, 'Yes.'

Before anything else, I have reached out to pals and close colleagues (I have no family) to put them in the picture. I did not want any lapses of memory or speech to be misinterpreted; I have always found it best to be clear and transparent. It takes the pressure off me by not trying to conceal any blunders. If I cannot find the name of the person or object, I openly whisper with a lifted eyebrow, 'That's the dementia' and carry on... To strangers, I just dismiss the memory slip with a wave of the hand and, 'Ha, it will come back later!'

Fortunately, the memory failure, which is still reasonably mild, takes on a strange form; I can often recall the first letter of the name or object, but not the name itself. For instance, the other day, I was discussing the suffragettes with lovely Susan and could not find the name of its lead protagonist. I knew it started with a P. Then, some ten or more minutes later, the name Pankhurst came to mind.

So far, my quality of life has only been affected by the fact that I can no longer drive; a former advanced driver, I am now unable to coordinate my moves. I have loved driving all my life and one of my biggest pleasures has been planning driving trips, with appropriate stops on the way to savour the local culture and sights. The planning was as much part of the fun as the drive itself. Sadly, this will no longer be possible.

One of the Greek philosophers (Plato, I believe, but I cannot be sure which one – call it early dementia!) likened memory to doves in a cage; occasionally, one of these elegant white birds is released and flies off into the sky. This beautiful metaphor is also giving me peace.

Once I know whether I have Alzheimer's or dementia, I will be able to embark on the necessary treatment (the former can be treated by medication; the latter cannot), including alternative therapies.

Taking a page from my coaching practice, as mentioned previously in having a choice and reframing your thoughts,[184] I have decided to do whatever I can that is within my control. I cannot reverse dementia (if that is what it is), but I *can* change my attitude towards it. Or, as Jean-Paul Sartre put it, 'Freedom is what you do with what's been done to you.'[185]

Assisted suicide is also a long-term option. This is something I have always considered and, in my living will, I made it clear – years ago – that, in the event of an accident, I was not to be resuscitated.

The support for euthanasia is gaining some traction with different religious leaders like Lord Carey, Rabbi Jonathan

---

184 See Chapter 3.

185 Jean Paul Sartre *Essays in Aesthetics* (2012, Open Road Media), p.11.

Romain, Archbishop Desmond Tutu and Reverend Rosie Harper. More recently, Dame Jenni Murray[186] and Lord Forsyth have come out supporting the 'Right To Die' campaign after witnessing their parents' suffering. One friend has gone even further and has made a pact with two girlfriends to undergo assisted suicide, in the event of succumbing to a debilitating incurable illness – even though they are breaking the (present) law.

Like Jenni Murray, I watched my mother's deterioration to Parkinson's, but, unlike Jenni, I offered to relieve my mother of her suffering, but she refused. She ended up surviving a heart attack (which affected her speech) and being admitted to a wonderful nursing home, Garside House, where she required 24-hour care and suffered memory loss and gradual paralysis over many years.

My father, who was struck by arthritis and vascular dementia (and the resulting mood swings), was very proud to have reached the age of ninety-three, but he had no quality of life. He kept falling and being admitted to A&E for his injuries.

As before, I have openly talked about this and four of my dearest friends have volunteered to accompany me to Switzerland (the only country which will permit this type of 'health tourism'). One of the early proponents for euthanasia,

---

186 https://www.dailymail.co.uk/femail/article-9718035/JENNI-MURRAY-right-die-pact-two-best-friends.html

and a dementia specialist, is Dr Colin Brewer,[187] whom I have known socially for over forty years; I have volunteered to help him with any research he is undertaking. Equally, I am registered at Chelsea and Westminster Hospital to take part in a new project where they are using a 3D camera to chronicle patients' facial expressions over time.

I know that assisted suicide will go against a lot of people's codes, but it is giving me back control of the situation. I know that, when I cease to operate normally and find daily chores a challenge, I have the option of making a polite exit from this world. With no family, I do not relish the thought of being treated by outsiders. I do not wish to embarrass myself with incontinence and an inability to communicate. The resilience that has resulted from my upbringing is serving me – and hopefully science – well. A positive thought to hang on to!

DO NOT LET AGE DEFINE YOU

'The right mindset, combined with perseverance and dedication, can create [new opportunities], regardless of age.'[188]

I have come to that blissful stage in life when I can have male friends without any confusion between sex, love and friendship. These lovely men (of which there are five or more)

---

187 Dr Colin Brewer, *O Let Me Not Ge Alzheimer's Sweet Heaven!* (Skyscraper Publications, 2019). See Chapter on Networking.
188 Som Bathla, *Mindset Makeover* (Amazon, 2021), p. 31.

are all younger than me by fifteen years or more. I have made it clear to two of them that I do not wish to enter into a physical relationship and that their friendship means more to me than a sexual one (which more often than not, in my case, often blurs the line). The friendship I have with these chaps is pleasantly different to the ones that I have with my female pals. I enjoy – and value – their male 'perspective'. To describe the difference would probably cover a second book, but I hope to have covered some of these issues in this book.

The benefit of hindsight – combined with some self-analysis – enables me to see things more clearly and to express myself without ambiguity. To quote the French poet, Nicolas Boileau,

'ce qui se conçoit bien s'énonce clairement, et les mots pour le dire arrivent aisément' – which is roughly translated as 'what is conceived well is clearly stated'.

I have learned so much and continue to learn something new every day. I attend webinars and events, which enlighten me and are where I make new connections. I believe that this curiosity translates itself into positive energy which, I am told, attracts people to me; especially, younger professionals.

This has resulted in a wonderful, enriching exchange; just as they learn from me, I learn from them. I also learn from my mistakes and, instead of dwelling on my failures and failings, I ask myself what I can do differently. Not 'SHOULD' have done differently, but 'WILL' do differently. It is, after all, the very essence of this book.

As I look back on my life, I am struck by three factors:

1. There is no doubt that Maxwell was a bully but he was prepared to take a risk by hiring me.

2. Maxwell's autocratic style had an advantage – it meant that whilst all decisions had to go through him, there was only ONE decision-maker.

3. I – who never had a coach or mentor – have been an active coach and mentor.

I have lost and regained my confidence.

I have had successes and failures. I have learnt to be kinder to myself and, in particular, to speak to myself as I would a friend – still a work in progress – but all positive steps forward. I have gone from being outwardly confident to inwardly confident.

ASK YOURSELF:

Of all the points raised in this book, which ones will you address first?

ASK YOURSELF 6 MONTHS FROM NOW:

What has changed in your life? And what further steps should you take to keep growing?

CONCLUSION

We can all learn from one another, and I hope *Stepping Into My Shoes* has given you food for thought.

A born egalitarian, I also hope it makes you more understanding towards your colleagues' and neighbours' 'otherness'.[189]

In their book *How Women Rise,* Sally Helgesen and co-author Marshall Goldsmith point to research carried out by Sally and her colleague, Julie Johnson,[190] and explain, 'how men place a greater value than women on winning…Women, by contrast… often went out of their way to describe winning as the result of a collaborative endeavour'.

In gaining a better understanding of your male and female colleagues, I hope you will break the divide between men and women and learn from each other – using communication techniques such as listening and even asking!

I also hope you will use this book and your notes as a Workbook – allowing yourself to reflect on the new techniques that you are going to try out, the new behaviours you are adopting and, above all, the new understanding you have gained of

---

189 Premuzic, p. 99.
190 Sally Helgesen and Marshall Goldsmith, *How Women Rise,* (Random House Business, 2018), p. 15.

yourself. I imagine you placing this book, with your completed ASK YOURSELF sections, on your bookcase or bedside and revisiting it to see what has changed since you turned the first page.

We are all different and that is great! By 'stepping into my shoes', you are encouraged to take one step at a time, but nothing is stopping you from starting today! All I ask of you is to be kind to yourself and kind to this *opus maximus* – there is a great deal of me in here; treat it with care.

Enjoy your journey, and thank you for listening to mine.

WHILE WE'RE ON THE SUBJECT...

TIME MANAGEMENT – MY WAY

I recently had a lovely house guest who commented on one of the good habits I learnt as a child, which was not wasting time by leaving the table empty-handed. For instance, if there were dirty plates to be taken away, I would do so there and then.

As my parents lived in a four-storey house, they developed a system whereby items placed on the right of the stairs were to go up and items on the left were to go down. Simple but effective.

Similarly, as mentioned previously under Dress for Success, I also learnt to prepare my satchel and books for the next day on the night before. This has kept me in good stead when preparing for a business meeting or a business trip; to this day, whenever possible, I always pack on the eve of the journey.

This time awareness has stayed with me ever since. For instance, there was a time when I set up my marketing consultancy. It was in the mid eighties and my first time without a secretary. It was also pre-internet so correspondence had to be sent by post. I developed routes to regular destinations knowing that I would come across a post box at a given street corner, and thereby killing two birds with one stone; on my way to my ultimate destination, I would place my correspondence in the pre-determined letter box.

Presently, I am juggling five 'jobs': writing this book, rebranding, coaching/mentoring, tutoring and working with a marketing expert. I look back on my days as a student when I had five days working on my thesis from 0900 to 1700, with no other responsibilities. Oh! Bring back those days!

Of course, my 'juggling' has nothing to do with the multi-tasking that career women who are also mothers have to deal with. It is a subject covered in many books, but probably best addressed by Mary Ann Sieghart in *The Authority Gap*, so I will not pretend to go there.

In order to appease my desire to make the most out of time, I have set up various systems:

I. Reading:
    I have two forms of reading – what I call my airport reading (such as James Patterson, Stephen Leather, Ian Rankin). These I list on an Excel sheet with comments. The reason for this is that publishers have a nasty habit of re-publishing the same book with a different cover. I hate wasting time, money and paper on repeat purchases.

    For my professional reading, I take notes as I go along, complete with page references, etc. These are then listed on an Index by subject, such as self-worth, procrastination, etc.

Time consuming you might say. Not for me as it enables me to write this book without having to go back to the book to find the relevant quote and location.

II. Contacts Book:
I address this in the Chapter on Networking.[191]

We all live 'crazy busy lives' to quote my friend and fellow coach, Zena Everett.[192] We meet a lot of people and may forget their names but remember where/ how you met them: by making notes such as 'Barefoot Conference', I can go through all cross references and easily find the person.

Clearly, as before, these entries are time-consuming but they are ultimately time-savers and obviate unnecessary stress.

III. Grocery Shopping:
I even write my weekly shop according to the layout of the supermarket!

IV. Cooking/Entertaining:
I used to entertain a lot, but less so of late. That said, when I do have friends round, I remain very aware of

---

191 See Chapter 9, *'When Networking is Connecting'*.
192 Zena Everett, *The Crazy Busy Cure* and her short 'productivity book' *Crazy Busy.*

the order in which ingredients should be prepared. For instance, can I make a dish the preceding day.

For me, entertaining six or more friends for a sit-down dinner need not be a source of panic; in fact, I devised a TV programme entitled Make a Meal of It in which the camera follows a host/hostess preparing a dinner – from shopping, cooking, to laying the table. My proposal did not go very far, but shortly afterwards, various TV shows were aired along the lines of Come Dine With Me, etc.

V. Arranging Diary Dates:
I increasingly use Calendly to allow both colleagues and friends to set up dates, and avoid a continuous back and forth on preferred times, locations and dates; one is Calendly for business, which automatically leads to a Zoom; the other is Calendly for friends.

In fact, effective time management for the self is the best way to increase your self-worth and welfare. Hill lists the key components to being kind to yourself:

- ► Make yourself a priority
- ► Say YES to yourself
- ► Find ways to save time
- ► Create a to-do list
- ► Use the time you have saved to do your task
- ► Create a daily routine

► Adjust your mindset
► Dedicate one day a month to you[193]

Establishing your new time management – like all changes – will not happen in one fell swoop. 'Change doesn't' happen overnight. Success is the sum of small efforts repeated day in and day out. If we make the effort, we will get better. If we don't, we won't.[194]

---

193 Hill, *Assertive Communication Skills*, pp 233-4.
194 Marshall Goldsmith, p.139.

DR CATHERINE'S TOP TIPS TO HAPPINESS

(The full version of the following was previously published in *Happiness* by *The Energy Healing Magazine*, 2022)

Happiness means different things to different people, but I would contend that happiness is not linked to material possessions. Happiness comes from within. Happiness is based on self-worth, NOT self-esteem; in other words it is not dependent on other's opinion of you. It also involves overcoming the obstacles that life might present you; for me, it is about regaining and maintaining control.

In my case, I was at the top of my career, securing a position at £75,000 (the equivalent of £225,000 today) in a completely new industry, becoming the first-ever European Business Director of the NASDAQ Stock Market, and then starting a company with a view to setting up solar parks on agricultural land in Italy... when everything fell apart: my elderly parents fell to Parkinson's (my mother), and dementia (my father). As their only child, I felt I had to take on their care – and did so. This meant giving up my new venture, particularly as I was the only Italian speaker amongst my partners.

This lasted nine relentless years in which I lost control of the most modest of 'commodities': my time. One minute, I was having a coffee with a friend (hoping for some semblance of 'normality'), the next I would be in an E&R (Emergency & Recovery) with one of my parents. There was no question of taking on work, of any kind.

It got to the point that I lost my identity. I recall consulting a wonderful psychotherapist and sitting down, in tears, declaring 'I do not know who I am anymore.' I relate all this only for you to understand how deep was my condition and would like to share with you how I gradually disentangled myself from the abysses of despair. So now, aged 69, I pass on to you how I found happiness.

Dr Catherine's Top Twelve Tips to Happiness

1. **YOU CANNOT ALWAYS CONTROL YOUR ENVIRONMENT.** If you do nothing else, realise you cannot change others and, sometimes, you are unable to alter your circumstances (think imprisonment here) – but you CAN change how you relate to your environment (and to other people). I recall that same psychotherapist asking me why I had given up my business venture and I could not find an answer. I have now learnt that I did not HAVE to give up the solar business venture and what I considered to be my filial duty was in fact MY CHOICE to assume (or not).

   One of my favourite films, *La Vità E Bella (Life Is Beautiful),* by the renowned Italian film maker, Roberto Benigni, further illustrates how your mindset impacts on your behaviour. In it, the main character, a Jewish Italian waiter, is deported with his family to the Auschwitz Concentration Camp and uses humour to shield his son from the horrors of their new 'home'. He pretends it is as a holiday camp and distorts all the statements from the Nazi Commanders as welcome statements to the new arrivals.

2. **YOU CANNOT CONTROL OTHERS. SO, FOCUS ON WHAT YOU CAN CHANGE AND EMBRACE THE CHANGE.** Have you heard yourself, or your best friend, say 'He/She is driving me mad'? 'I wish they could change'. Well, the bad news is that they are not likely to change, and you are most unlikely to change them – BUT the good news is that you can change your attitude towards them. Perhaps you do not like how your spouse grinds their teeth when eating their cereals. Do you really think you can alter their life-long (involuntary) habit? No, but you can change is your reaction. Think about it! Once you rid yourself of your irritation, you will be much freer...

3. **FREE YOURSELF FROM OTHER PEOPLE'S OPINON.** Stop being reliant on what they think of you. Feedback is one thing, particularly when we are learning, but freedom can be gained when you cease to depend on others' view of you. As you free yourself from the shackles of their opinion, you can concentrate on being yourself, warts and all.

4. **STOP PEOPLE-PLEASING.** We are polite people
   and we do not like to say 'No'. However, we cannot
   accept everything. Mercifully, you can learn to decline
   a request, without being rude. Saying NO is not a
   sign of ill-breeding or aggression if delivered in the
   right way; in fact, it signals your assertiveness. Rather
   than express a straight NO, offer a half-way solution
   – such as 'I cannot do a full day, but I could offer
   you 2 hours.' Or, you may use a deferring technique,
   requesting more time to make a decision. As long
   as you take into consideration the other person's
   feelings, you are not being offensive.

   For too long, I have been all too willing to help people
   out, even if it meant my giving up an activity or
   somehow complicating my life. It has taken me years
   to realise that I should curb my eagerness to please/
   come to the rescue. Not only was this volunteering
   impacting on my work and my leisure time, it often
   was not really helping the person in question, because
   what they often REALLY needed was to find a solution
   for themselves, rather than assistance from the likes of
   me.

5. **LEARN TO EXPRESS YOURSELF TO AVOID
   CONFRONTATION.** Break free from emotional
   outbursts. Messages and emotions do not mix. Have
   you ever found yourself so upset/angry that you are
   unable to communicate your thoughts? And instead
   of saying what you want to convey, you shout and

maybe even scream – to no avail. This is where preparation comes into play.

Start by considering WHAT you wish to convey and TO WHOM, and WHEN – then PRACTICE. In doing so, you will let go of your resentment/anger/sadness and make way for your journey to happiness.

6. **VOICE YOUR FEELINGS.** It took me years to learn this. I stupidly believed that my husband and close friends could read my discontent, without my uttering a single word. But why should they? They were not mind-readers! So, I started to say things (always in the first person) like 'When you do this, I feel ....' I also expressed these thoughts in a way that encouraged a dialogue between us. This did not happen overnight but it was well worth it.

   As Ant Middleton, the former Special Services soldier and presenter of *SAS: Who Dares Wins* puts it, 'the long-term consequences of putting up with things will far outweigh the short-term discomfort of confrontation'.

7. **SET BOUNDARIES.** Boundaries are not about keeping people out, but about communicating with improved clarity and maintaining each other's values and needs. By setting boundaries with your colleagues/partners, you are telling them what works for/with you and what does not; you are defining how far they can

go and – also – where not to go... Boundaries only become valid if you realise you have choices; you do not HAVE to be available 24 hours a day. Boundaries are about saying NO and not feeling guilty.

How do you know when you need to set up boundaries? When:

- ► You feel your colleagues/partners are taking advantage of you
- ► You feel that your job/life consists of responding to other people's messages and calls
- ► You feel you have lost control of your time and you are spending too much time dealing with other people's needs
- ► You are trying to help in matters which are beyond your control.

8. **USE HUMOUR.** Humour is one of my pet subjects, particularly in the context of regaining control or defusing a tense situation. Many a comedian has admitted they used humour to turn the table very early in life when dealing with their contemporaries in the playground. [See Sir Lenny Henry's story in the chapter on Humour in this book.]

In my case, humour is my 'mask' which enables me to conceal my shyness. It is like a form of armour that shields me and enables me to go forth into what I call the 'corporate jungle'. It also works in all forms of relationships, but is particularly useful in the workplace.

A word of caution here: humour is a difficult 'tool' to play, so awareness of your 'audience' is a prime consideration.

9. **BE KIND TO YOURSELF**. Now that you have learnt to say NO, you have also given yourself time and space to look after yourself. Still unsure? Try speaking to yourself as you would to your best friend. You might even like to practice 'The Chair Technique' that is often used in coaching: place a chair in front of you and address the chair as if it was occupied by your best friend.

10. **LET GO OF THE PAST AND LOOK FORWARD TO THE FUTURE. DO NOT HOLD ON TO YOUR MISTAKES – LEARN FROM THEM**. Rid yourself of guilt and regret. As Thomas Edison famously said, 'I have not failed. I've just found 10,000 ways that won't work.' Ignore SNAFUs[195] and focus on the future.

By the same token, holding onto grudges is another impairment that serves no good, other than to eat you up inside. In the words of Shakespeare, 'What's done is done'.

---

195 SNAFU is a term invented by American soldiers in Vietnam meaning, 'Situation Normal All Fxxxxed Up'.

'Life changes for the better when you prioritize how your life feels than how it looks' (Anon).

11. **STOP SEEKING PERFECTION.** 'To err is human'. In the same way as I suggested earlier not to look at yourself in the light of what others think of you, do not compare yourself to others. Realise that your best IS your best.

12. **AVOID PROCRASTINATION.** Buying time and procrastination are not the same thing. Whilst you may need time to reflect, there is a point at which you must put an end to the 'reflection'. I have told you that my friends say that the 'A' in my name stands for 'Action Woman'. I hope that this does not mean I am reckless but there is a side of me which feels 'there is no point in delaying matters, let us go ahead'. Consider what you have to lose if you do not move forward.

The other aspect for me as 'Action Woman' is that, if I fail to act on a point – no matter how trivial – it remains as 'Outstanding'.

13. **GET RID OF NEGATIVE THOUGHTS – SURROUND YOURSELF WITH POSITIVE PEOPLE.** Remember, negativity breeds negativity. Avoid the doom-mongers. I liken it to attaching yourself to a sinking ship. Why would you do that?

14. **MAINTAIN YOUR CURIOSITY AND APPETITE FOR THE PRESENT.** I get up every morning and learn something new every day, regardless of my age.

15. **LEARN HUMILITY.** The Corporate Philosopher Professor Roger Steare promotes the notion of the three HUMs in leadership, but they also apply in my view to our daily way of life:

   ► **HUM**ility
   ► **HUM**anity
   ► **HUM**our

   In the words of another philosopher, 'Know you do not know'.

16. **DO NOT RUN AWAY**. Wherever you go, you take your baggage with you. Travel can be a wonderful tool for learning more about yourself – especially travelling solo. But it is not an escape. Wherever you go, you take your luggage with you. Look at what you are REALLY avoiding and can change.

Few changes take place without S-T-E-P-S, which is why patience and being kind to yourself are important components in attaining happiness. In the same way that an Olympic athlete has to train to achieve the necessary degree of excellence required to win, so too these changes take time and perseverance.

Dr Catherine A. Baudino

CONTACT THE AUTHOR

After her successful career in the corporate world, Dr Catherine Baudino is now an executive coach, mentor and writer, where she further develops on the subjects outlined in this book.

- ► To learn more about Dr Catherine, secure a free 30 minute consultation or obtain further copies of her book, visit her website at www.drcatherinecoaching. com
- ► All comments and enquiries welcome at enquiries@ drcatherinecoaching.com

COMMENTS FROM CLIENTS

Catherine is not a common mentor. What makes Catherine 'special' is her immense knowledge, a brilliant entrepreneurial attitude, an inimitable class, and an outstanding sense of humour too. During her tailored mentoring program I have learnt the following:

- to always do the right thing,
- to value others and help them whenever I can,
- to always plan ahead, work hard and do my best in any situation,
- to be a life-long learner; to smile and keep a sense of humor even when things get tough,
- and to love, support and protect the person I love most.

Furthermore, she not only helped me to grow as a person, but she also indirectly showed me that: nothing is impossible if you want it.

Federico Meoni, Analyst, Finance

I have worked closely with Catherine for the past few years as a client of her business as well as her being a client of mine. The professionalism and dedication of this remarkable woman is second to none; in these years in which we have worked together I have received the most valuable advice which can only come from very special kind of individual. Catherine has proven time and time again totally spot on with her vision and ability to foresee obstacles that might hinder success in the short term as well as in the long haul So... the journey continues...

Miguel Arrantes-Galvao, Faintline Digital Artistry

Dr Catherine is very nice and approachable. She's also firm with a clear process to get us up and running. She's so diligent that she even responds to her client out of the usual working hours with helpful ideas, information and advice. Additionally, I would venture that her services border on those of a business strategist and would recommend Dr Catherine's services every time.

Lily G Stress Reliever

BIBLIOGRAPHY

Aaker Jennifer, and Naomi Bagdonas *Why Humor is a Secret Weapon in Business and Life and How Anyone Can Harness It, Even You* (Currency, 2020)

Babcok, Linda and Laschever, Sara, *Women Don't Ask* (Princeton University Press, 2021)

Baker, Wayne, *All You Have to Do Is Ask* (Currency, 2020)

Bathla, Som, *Mindset Makeover* (Amazon, 2021)

Beard, Mary, *Women & Power* (Profile Books, 2017)

Bergson, Henri, *Le Rire* (7th edition. Paris, Felix Alcan, 1911)

Brescoll, VL, 2011, *Who Takes the Floor and Why* (Administrative, Science Quarterly, Vol. 56, No 4)

Brewer, Dr Colin, *O Let Me Not Ge Alzheimer's Sweet Heaven!* (Skyscraper Publications, 2019)

Bündchen, Giselle, *Lessons* (Avery, 2018)

Bunting, Nicola, Dr, *Who Do You Want to Be? How To Embrace Change and Live Your Dream* (Platkus, 2012)

Carroll, Lewis, *Father William*

Charmirri-Premuzic, Tomas, *Why Do so Many Incompetent Men Become Leaders? (and How to Fix It)* (Harvard Business Review Press)

Clifton, Rita, *Love Your... Imposter* (Kogan Page, 2020)

Daily Mail - https://www.dailymail.co.uk/tvshowbiz/article-2380539/Kristin-Scott-Thomas-I-invisible-like-middle-aged-women.html

https://www.dailymail.co.uk/femail/article-9917137/Meet-Britains-heeled-women-Meet-shoe-addicts-giving-Imelda-Marcos-run-money.html

Dweck, Carole, Dr, *Mindset – Changing the Way You Think to Fulfil Your Potential* (Robinson, 2017)

Everett, Zena, *The Crazy Busy Cure* (Nicholas Brealey Publishing, 2021) and her short 'productivity book' *Crazy Busy*.

Feller, Bruce, *Life is in The Transitions* (Penguin Press, 2020)

Goldsmith, Marshall, *Triggers* (Profile Books, 2016)

Sylvia Ann Hewlett and Carolyn Buck Luce

Frankl, PhD, Lois, *Nice Girls Do Not Get the Corner Office* (Business Plus, 2014)

HBR's 10 Must Reads, *On Women and Leadership* (2019)

Ibarra Herminia, *Working Identity* (Harvard Business Press, 2003)

Halliday, Tara, *Unmasking: The Coach's Guide to Imposter Syndrome* (Rethink Press, 2018)

Helgesen, Sally and Marshall Goldsmith, *How Women Rise* (Random House Business, 2019)

Hibberd, Dr Jessamy, *The Imposter Cure* (Aster, 2019)

Hill, Grace, *Assertive Communication Skills* (2021)

James, Judi, *Being Confident* (Vermillion, London, 2011)

Johnson, Charysse, LCMHC, NCC *Expired Mindsets* (NDP, 2021)

King, Patrick, *The Art of Witty Banter, Be Quick, Be Clever, Quick & Magnetic* (Amazon, 2022)

Lawson, Charles, *The Unnatural Networker* (Panoma Press, 2014)

Dr Henry Mark, *Positive Boundaries at Workplace* (Amazon, 2021)

Martin, Sharon, https://www.livewellwithsharonmartin.com/set-boundaries-toxic-people/

Max Mason, *Stop Doubting Yourself* (Amazon, 2021)

Middleton, Ant, *Mental Fitness* (Harper Collins, 2021)

Zero Negativity (Harper Collins, 2021)

Misner, Ivan, *Networking Like a Pro* (Entrepreneur Press, 2010)

Murray, Jenni, https://www.dailymail.co.uk/femail/article-9718035/JENNI-MURRAY-right-die-pact-two-best-friends.html

Portas, Mary, *Work Like a Woman* (Penguin, 2018)

Rogers, Carl R., and Richard Evans Farson, *Active Listening* (Mansfield Centre: Martino Publishing, 1957)

Sartre, Jean-Paul, *Essays in Aesthetics* (2012, Open Road Media)

Robin Sharma, *The Leader Who Had No Title* (2010)

Sieghart, Mary Ann, *The Authority Gap* (Penguin, 2022)

Smith, James, *NOT A Life Coach* (Harper Collins Publishers, 2020)

Tannen PhD, Deborah, *Talking 9 To 5* (William Morrow and Company, 1994)

Turnbull, James, *The Essential Guide to Assertiveness* (libritopublising, 2021)

Unerman, Sue and Jacob, Kathryn, *The Glass Wall* (Profile Books, 2016)

Welck Karl E., *Small Wins: 'Reflecting the Scale of Social Problems', American Psychologist 39, no 1* (January, 1984)

Williams James W., *Listening Skills Training* (Amazon, 2021)

Whitty-Collins, Gill, *Why Men Win at Work* (Luath Press Ltd, p. 2021)

Wosskow, Debbie and Anna Jones, *Believe, Build and Become* (Virgin Books, 2019)

Young Ed. D, Valerie, *The Secret Thoughts of Successful Women* (Crown Business, 2011)

Zahariades, Damon, *The Art Saying No* (Art of Productivity, 2017)